Beckery Burrows

Beckery Burrows

Somerset in the Thirties

by RAY BURROWS

WITH A FOREWORD BY
MARTYN BROWN

THE RESEARCH PUBLISHING CO.
52 LINCOLN'S INN FIELDS · LONDON

To my favourite 'foreigner'
SYLV
my London-born wife

publication of this book has been assisted by a grant from
C. & J. Clark Ltd, Street, Somerset

ISBN 0 7050 0054 0 (hard-back)
ISBN 0 7050 0055 9 (limp)
Printed in Gt Britain for The Research Publishing Co.
(Fudge & Co., Ltd.), London.

Contents

Foreword

It is surprising how much history, and even modest history, has been written from the position of those charged with running, or attempting to run, our lives, and how little from the real life experience of people themselves. History has been concerned with rulers, and their governments, laws and Acts, battles and reforms. Even the history of the labour movement has been written from the vantage point of trades union officials and the minutes of their meetings.

The reason for this emphasis has been explained by the historian's reliance on the survival of documents and manuscripts as his source material. In recent years the techniques have altered and the growth of interest in local history and local people has encouraged the use of first hand memories of the past. *Larkrise to Candleford* and *Akenfield* represent two contrasting studies of village communities and the changes that have taken place within them in living memory. The speed of change has emphasized the value of recording the old, and not so old, people who can frequently recall events and attitudes which seem more akin to medieval life than to the 20th century.

Ray Burrows has written his view of life from the fringe of Glastonbury in the 1930s. The book vividly recaptures the essence, or perhaps the odour, of the times and links social comment with sharp detail.

Martyn Brown,
Keeper of Rural Life,
Somerset Rural Life Museum,
Glastonbury,
Somerset.

IN AVALON

The Abbot was Landlord.
The Abbot was Law.
The Abbey was famed
'Richest Abbey of All'.

'Why', asked the Pilgrim,
'Do you not care
For this green Isle
Midst hallowed air?'

'I care', quoth the Man,
'For this, that you see,
Are the workfields of life,
. . . and the death of me.

'These historical buildings
Of days long gone by,
Were built, and were tended
By kin such as I.

'But pray take your fill
Of this awe that you need.
I can tarry no longer.
I have young mouths to feed.'

Introduction

I was born and raised in rural Somerset when towns and villages had their boundaries, and one was made to feel a 'foreigner' when moving from place to place.

My Somerset life ended in 1943, when I joined the Royal Navy for a fourteen year period, and during this time the only changes apparent to me were the changes in the Royal Navy.

'There is nothing strange about that,' you may think, 'That type of thing happened to lots of people.' Yes, that is quite true, but there's another thing.

On returning to my home town, I found that things had changed too rapidly for me. I had travelled, but I had always had a driver who knew where he was going. Life was a huge, strange rush. The horse and cart had gone, and cars and lorries were here to stay. The old values had changed. A crumpled horn was once used to denote a certain cow—whereas any old horn on any old cow would be a novelty these days. I used to love haymaking. The horses, the haywains, the picks, the hayricks, the handrakes—and here were tractors, mechanisation and bales.

There were more buildings, different people—different-sounding people, and I was constantly drawn to the old folk to hear the sounds I wanted to hear. Some of these looked quite at home behind the wheel of a car and seemed quite unperturbed with the speed and hustle and bustle.

Modern traffic on the old roads. There was no room for me on that old bike of mine. Lorries passed too closely, and their extra long beds and trailers startled me into the gutter or onto the grass verge. Whatever happened to those old short lorries?

I decided to change, too. I bought a scooter. This changed things—far too rapidly for me to cope with. I sold it a week later.

About seven years ago I learnt to drive a car. I had joined them. I had arrived! Monte Carlo, here I come! Well, not really . . .

I couldn't even find Montacute—sixteen miles from where I had been born! 'It will pass' . . . 'You will get used to it,' they said. Then why did I have to make three attempts to find Baltonsborough (4 miles)?—

I could have got there the first time across the fields! Is Cadbury, like
Camelot, no more than a legend? . . . No? . . . Then why is it never
there when I arrive? True, I found Keinton Mandeville (5 miles) and
Castle Cary (10 miles) on the way, but both places had removed themselves to Barton St David on the return trip, thus foiling me from finding the home road.

'What about a map?'

Ah, yes . . . I have survey maps of Somerset, ordnance maps of
Somerset, road maps of Somerset, maps of the Somerset motorways,
two maps with the Somerset and Dorset Railway on them. You name it,
I've got it. They're handy. They show you *where* to go, but not *how*.
They show where a place *is*, but fail to show you the complications of
that place. Take Castle Cary for instance. Look at the map. You will
observe there are a lot of roads *leading into* Cary, yet, in actual practise,
I find that all exit routes lead to Shepton Mallet (9 miles)! This does
sound silly, I know, but I have proved it to be true on three occasions.

I have heard drivers relate their tales of driving on the Continent.
I tell them of the time I drove to Blackford. 'Blackford?' they exclaim.
'Yes, Blackford,' I reply—I didn't intend to go there, mind. I was trying to find Burtle (8 miles) at the time. Blackford—nine miles from
home and I had never heard of the place until I arrived there! It seems
that every time the Glastonbury Tor drops out of sight I get an old
feudal feeling that I shouldn't be where I am at that moment.

I approached Old Stan'l who drives a car despite his similar up-
bringing to mine.

'How do you get on with driving a car, Stan?' I asked him.

'Well, now,' said Stan, ''Tis alright for mugglen about in round home,
but it ain't no good if you do want to go somewhere in p'ticular, if you
do see what I mean, do 'ee?'

See?

Oh, I do, Stan—I do!

Street, 1978   R. B.

BRIEF GLOSSARY

Somerset	Standard English	Somerset	Standard English
ah	yes	um	they, them, those
'ee	you	un	him, one
gert	great	ur	he, it
thiick	that		

Before, and to Start With

It was in mid-Somerset in the late 1920s when I let loose my first bawl as to 'the many my maybes', and laid claim to my share of inheritance of the Isle of Avalon.

My two and a half-year old, elder brother was probably too young to notice. Our Vather most likely accepted it as a signal to get more drunk than usual. And I'm sure Our Mother thanked God that that lot was over, and settled down for a quiet snooze.

I surveyed my surroundings, which consisted of a bed made in one of the drawers from the 'chester drawers' upstairs, and was highly delighted to find that Uncoo Awfie had the good sense to own an Airedale bitch who considered herself one of the family.

Gramf patted his 'maid' on the head, smiled kindly towards me, and then returned to his waiting horse and cart (property of the Somerset and Dorset Joint Railway). Our Auntie Vere got on with the cleaning up, sparing a few comforting words for me now and again.

What else had I got? There was the great outdoors—not *all* of it, mind. No, my share ended at the boundaries of Beckery, and . . . Where? Beck . . . Oh. I can see I shall have to be a little more explicit. We are surrounded by miles and miles of flat, green, moor—the Somerset Flats. Way back along, it was once possible to sail in from the high seas over these moors—so our present day hills would have been islands then. This area consisted of three islands. The largest one was Glastonbury. Celtic name, YNYSWYTRYN, the Crystal Isle. A Celtic name from the Celtic legend of their Hereafter in the Happy Hunting Grounds—a Crystal Tower in the Heavens. Why? Well, if you stood on a high vantage point and saw the mist-covered Moors surrounding the foot of the 520-foot Glastonbury Tor, you would get a rough idea of its origin.

Glastonbury. Gateway to Christianity in the West. Joseph of Aramathea is said to have landed on Weary All Hill just after the Crucifixion. He stuck his staff in the ground . . . said, 'Weary all', and slept . . . the staff took root, to grow into the Holy Thorn . . . and Joseph of Aramathea later buried the Holy Chalice in some unknown place in Glastonbury.

1

The second largest island was about two miles away. Street. Celtic name, LLANTOKAL, the Church of Tecla. St Tecla worked in the German area, so why? — I don't know. Well, these old saints *did* travel about quite a lot, didn't they? Take St Indract, for instance. During his travels, he and seven of his companions decided to call in at Glastonbury to see St Patrick's tomb. Their staves were tipped with brass. The natives of Shapwick thought it was gold, and murdered all eight of them for it.

This, of course, has nothing to do with Street, but it does show that travelling *was* travelling in those days, and that Shapwick natives were not then 'on their metal' on metal. Street was later called LEGA. I can't explain this either; Lega—a league?—About three miles long? (Honestly, I could never understand how a Somerset man can possibly be a student of Latin, or of any other foreign language.)

The smallest island was between the other two, and about three quarters of a mile from Glastonbury—Beckery. It was used as a settlement for the monks before they were appointed to their duties at the Abbey. Most of the monks travelled from Waterford—Bristol—Beckery. In Waterford Harbour there is a small island called BEG ERI—Little Ireland, and Beckery is said to derive from this name. It's plausible, I suppose. Give us a foreign word or name, and we'll soon make mincemeat out of it around here. Take 'Aquaduct', for instance. We have an area near here called 'Acky Dock' which used to have 'some sort of a bridge there at one time'.

A main road now runs from Glastonbury to Street, tightly hugging the toes of Weary All, and brushing past Morland's Factory, seemingly to keep away from Beckery as much as possible, so we found ourselves on a loop-road which travelled from the bottom end of Glastonbury, past the junction of the railway and the moor roads, up through Beckery, through Baily's Factory, and then joined the main road on the other side of Morland's Factory at Northover. Of course, our road became known as 'Down round the Back'. No harm meant, and none taken, for we knew where we lived.

Far away, somewhere on the other side of Weary All, a Cut was dug from a bend in the River Brue to carry water alongside Morland's, under Baily's, behind the stone houses in Beckery, under Snow's Timber Yard and the cross-line gates of the railway, and from there out into the moor to rejoin the Mother Brue on her long trip to Burnham. The road and the Cut 'Down round the Back' wended side by side like two old friends, embracing as the road bridged the water at Baily's, and then continued their double paths to the railway and moor roads junction.

A field away from Baily's, Beckery sat on either side of the road. A row of red brick houses on one side, and a row of grey stone houses on the other. On the factory-end of the stone houses was a cottage with church-kind of windows. On the other side of the river, behind the stone houses, was a burnt out mill. It had been burnt down before I was born, thus making it the one major accident down our way for which I was not blamed. There were three more houses in the vicinity of the mill, linking them up with the far end of Baily's Factory. We weren't allowed near these, and we tended to look upon them as 'not belonging' to the rest of us.

There you have it. Two rows of houses in a tidy heap, surrounded by fields, bordering on the edges of the moor.

With such a small portion of green, pleasant, land to call my own, one could automatically consider the advantages of all this country-fresh air. There wasn't a lot of that about, neither! Baily's Factory 'did' sheepskins and made 'tennis-bats'. Just behind Baily's the property of Morland's commenced, and it was here they dug deep pits in the ground and filled them with effluent sludge from their factory, who 'done' sheep-skins in a bigger way. It became so successful it was made into one large lake, and was soon dubbed 'Morland's Lagoon'. I am not saying it smelled. It stank! The aroma was improved by the heat of the summers when the taste became worse than the smell. It was so thick and heavy that flies made a meal of it. This is the only explanation I can give for the plague of flies in our house, because we didn't have enough spare food to feed *that* many. Winter time was much better. There were no flies and the smell was less potent, but the damp mists and drizzly rain would hold the half-as-bad-smell to our clothing and we would carry an unwanted supply to the complaining citizens Up Town.

Our fine breeding made us sensitive. A man with a genuine cold could get thumped in the ear-hole for sniffing in our presence.

All was forgiven, though, when the Lagoon froze over to make a marvellous skating rink. Even the blokes, with their skates from Up Town, came down our way for that. Of all the hundreds who skated on there, only one fell through. Nothing serious. He was numb with the cold, but he could take it. The cuts and grazes from the broken ice didn't even bother him—but the smell almost killed him! I can still see him now—up to his chest in broken ice, surrounded by would-be rescuers who were all very adept in the art of pulling sheep, cows and horses out of a ditch, but unable to get close enough to him . . . and he, only four feet from

the bank. Naturally, he had to walk home . . . Not even a putt would
carry that type of load.

Beckery folk shopped, went to school, and paid their dues in Glastonbury, and the slightest wayward step from the recognised paths would
be quickly greeted with a quizzical 'Hello. What's he doing here, then?'
from all sides, for our feudal boundaries were closely observed. We
received the same treatment from the Street folk, who would also add
insult to injury by classifying us under the general heading of 'that
Glastonbury lot'.

The moor folk (bless them), in their lives of isolation, made even
closer boundaries because they distinguished between moor folk and
moor folk—where the end of one field and the starting of another could
be a different story altogether. Their suspicious, hostile attitude to the
'foreigner', the outsider, filled me with warmth, for there I received the
same treatment as the rest. Equality at last!

The Beckery boundaries were seldom breached. As I said before, we
lived 'Down round the Back', and who'd want to go down there apart
from the Beckeryites?

Most people tend to look upon the Somerset country folk as slow,
simple, peaceful, comical rustics. Now, I wonder? We don't mind
them thinking this, because it enables us to take advantage of the unsuspecting more easily, should the need arise. We *do* speak slowly, but
we manage to keep apace with the modern agricultural surroundings—
and, with a little thought,—one must realise that it takes a keen eye and
an alert mind actually to *watch the grass grow*. 'If you want to say something—say something worthwhile. If you say something worthwhile—
enjoy *the saying of it*.'

The peace and quiet of a country town became disrupted at the turn
of this century when the local folk attempted to hang a policeman on
Street Cross because he 'kept on comin' it a bit much', (too officious).
The culprits fled over to Wales. Why go there? Because it happened to
be the nearest place—too far away for the local Bobby on his bike. Poor
old Wales? . . . Not really, because they used to send their blokes over
here—and I had an Uncoo Taff to prove this. (Nice little bloke, he was.
Married our Aunt Ider, he did, and we all felt so sorry for him.)

At about the same time, a policeman attempted to stop some citizens
of Street from performing the ancient rites of a Skimmington Dance.
(Also locally referred to as a Skimmerton Ride and a Skirmidging Trundle.
Perm any three by three for the safest bet.) 'Wife' or 'husband swapping'

was not what it is today, and the local folk would voice their disapproval
by turning out in force to rattle pots and pans, and to sing and shout
around the house in which the lovers' tryst took place. Puritanical
views? . . . No. From what I gather, it was a chance of a booze-up and
to let off steam. As Old Bert once informed me, 'There were probably
a bit of jealousy about it. You know, somebody gettin' a bit more than
t'other.' Anyroad, the policeman was pushed through a window for his
trouble, and some of the dancers and onlookers were sent to Shepton
Mallet jail.

In the late 1800s the folk of Hillhead, Glastonbury practised the
noble art of 'Tail Piping'. What? – You've never heard of it? Please allow
this country lad to explain. Hillhead was a tough-spot of Glastonbury in
those days and the local police had to go there in twos. Had an ill-advised
Bobby gone there alone, the Hillhead folk would crowd around him in
order to place a rolled newspaper spiel up under his belt from behind–
and then set fire to it! Happily, this no longer happens, thus sparing an
embarrassed Bobby from making a 999 call without knowing which
emergency service he required the most urgently.

Please don't think that violence among the Somerset folk applied
only to Glastonbury and Street. Another Street pensioner, who had
spent his childhood in Crewkerne, told me,

'There was a place there called Lye Water, and it seemed as though
there was always a fight going on there'.

'A lot of rough blokes, were they, Ernie?' I prompted.

'Blokes?' he replied–'I'm talking about the women!'

I think our old-fashioned dialect has a lot to do with the comical
character we tend to portray. It is one of the most perfect remains of
the Anglo-Saxon language (the stuff used in King Alfie's court), and
thee would'st not laugh at just an old-fashioned tongue, would'st? We
went to school just like anyone else, but we treat Standard English as
we would any other foreign language.

Here are a few of the many Anglo-Saxon words we use in dialect.

Standard	Dialect	Anglo-Saxon
against	agen	agen
stay	bide	bidan
egg	agg	aeg
crows	craws	crawe
twilight	dimpsy	dimse

Standard	Dialect	Anglo-Saxon
elm	elum	ellm
gate	geat	geat
half	haaf	healf
wrist	han'wrist	hand-wyrst
roost	hroost	hrost
short sharp hill	knap	cnaep
that	thiik	thylic

We are not only masters of the seemingly-common double-negative, but of the triple and quadruple negative as well, and we don't never seem to say nothing proper. We know what we mean, but it comes out differently.

'Shall I say it louder, if thee can'st not hear me?'

'If thee art not talking to I, why dost thee not say so?'

'If you'm going to keep on startling folk like that, thee should'st warn 'em first!'

'Did'st thee see anybody asking for I today?'

And we laugh at the Irish with the rest of you.

We like to use words to describe the sound of things. An unoiled wheel in need of axle grease 'quirks'. To 'retch' is to 'urge'. Footsteps 'squelch' as one walks through 'soggy and squodgey' marshland. We 'hump' to 'carry' because it necessitates the bending of the back—grunting to lift.

We sometimes use an 'z' for an 's', and a 'v' for an 'f'. They are pronounced in a sort of half-tone value, mostly. 'Six folk of Somerset' would be pronounced as 'Zix volk o' Zummerzet', and the 'z' in 'zix' would sound much harder than the two in Zummerzet.

We drop the 'w' from the beginning of some words. 'Wood' becomes ''ood'. 'Would'st' becomes ''ood'st'. 'Weather' remains 'weather', and 'water' becomes 'wadder'. The lost 'ws' are re-employed on words like 'whome' for 'home', and 'wold' meaning 'old'.

A word commencing with 'r' is usually preceded with a throat-sounding 'h'. Hrain. Hrake. Hroad. Hrun. 'Hran' does not come into this group very often, because the past tense of 'run' is 'runned', and instead of saying 'hrunned' we say 'hurned', a sort of cross between 'runned' and 'hurried'.

A strange progression, isn't it? Let's have a look at another one. 'With you'—'with thee'—'wi' thee'—'withee'—'bithee'. What is that 'b' doing there?—I don't know. It probably comes from another word which has lost one. 'Behind'–'vehind'. Try looking at it the other way. 'Oven' becomes 'ubben'. 'Even' becomes 'eb'n'. 'Gert' means 'great', which is 'perty' obvious, isn't it? There are other words that come from no-where in particular, yet sound so right in application. A daft (or 'dunch') gert 'lummox' . . . A lazy gert 'lummick' . . . A 'slummick' can mean both, or either of them. 'Slummicky' is 'slack' or 'sagging' or 'under the weather' or 'out of sorts'. A 'momet' is a 'scarecrow', but a 'mommick' is an object of annoyance.

Has any of this puzzled you up to now?–Now *that* is a good word. 'Puzzle'. 'Puzzle' is 'puggoo', but only in the mind, because a puzzle remains a puzzle, and every maze a puzzle-garden. One could be said to be 'puggoo'd-drunk', 'knocked-puggoo'd', or just 'puggoo'd'. 'Puggoo-headed' folk will not listen to reason, and the 'puggoo-minded' ones are unable to reason with what they hear.

'Puggoo' should never be confused with 'muggoo'. Now, 'a muggoo' *is* 'a muddle'. A 'right, or tidy old muggoo' can be a tangle or a mess. To 'muggoo-on'–you carry on. To 'muggoo-on on your own'–you manage. To be 'mugglen-on'–you resume your journey, because 'mugglen' means travelling. So, 'fair to mugglen' *has* to mean 'Not too bad, thank you', doesn't it?

Of course, it is pretty obvious that all this careful explanation has been leading up to a test. Any non-Somerset person who manages to read the following three sentences without a falter has my permission to address any member of my family as 'me dear'.

1. You cannot see as well as you could, can you?–You have to wear glasses, do you not?
2. Thee cans't not see as well as thou could'st, cans't not?–Thee hast to wear glasses, hast thou not?
3. Thee cassn't zee az well az coost, cast?–Thees't gotta wear glassies, hassn't?

There's simple Somerset brevity for you–isn't it?

There was one other character common to the Somerset man in the thirties, and they were all drunk at sometime or another. The medical profession and Alcoholics Anonymous will quote today's statistics and inform us that alcoholism is on the increase. Have they, I wonder, allowed for the drift from this area to theirs?–We used to see hundreds of drunks every day! Not for us those ordinary ale-swilling topers of town life–for ours were the cider-drunks of the worst kind! Do I mean alcoholics? No, I don't, because those were the days when only the rich

had nervous breakdowns, the poor just had bad nerves, and teatotallers
were something to be sneered at.

The drunks were so many and varied we had to have a titled list for
them.

Theirs	*Ours*
D.Ts. (delirium tremens)	Do-ally-tap
Prospective candidate for above	Touch of the do-ally-tap
Either of the above two	Puggoo'd-drunk
Drunk and disorderly	Wild-haring-drunk
Drunk and incapable	Blind-zozzled
Too drunk to be either	Stooded
Just drunk	Three-parts slewed
Tipsy	Skimmished
Merry	Market fresh

Now, Our Vather was a heavy drinker. Cider had no notable effect
on his mind because he started off with less brain than nil. If anything,
the cider most probably doubled the size of the vacuum inside his head,
for he existed within, and solely for himself. Of all the drunks in
Somerset, we had to have the one in our house who had earnt the nickname of 'Swiggy'. Now, that's fame for you! His nickname wasn't
'family', so I decided to check up on its origin. To drink from a bottle?—
To swig?—Swiggy? It didn't take long, and I was almost right.

Was he a great drinker? I can't honestly say, as I only drank with him
when he was on the decline of old age—when a couple of pints would
send him into the same lying-story-filled rut where nothing went right
and everything was done in a personal attempt to upset him. The
Second World War was one of these items, because the Home Guard
duties spoilt his best night out on Fridays.

It seems that Vather, in his youth, rented himself out to Varmer
Blaker on one of his dole-days to help with the haymaking, and Vather,
being the greedy, self-centred swine he'd always been, spent more time
with the 'wooden bottle' (firkins,—small barrels of cider), and sadly
neglected his duties of the old-fashioned style of haymaking. (Hard
labour was another name for it if one was unaccustomed to the work.)

Varmer Blaker had to send back to the farm for extra firkins of cider
to appease the genuine workers, and so decided to teach Vather a lesson.

Varmer Blaker was a huge, jolly, fat man who loved cider and playing practical jokes. His cider was as rough as the playing of his jokes, but

lacked the subtle, cunning touches he employed to trap his unsuspecting victims. Either way, they finished up with a bad head. He had once bet Ernie Gigg something about a certain local horse, and vowed that, should he be proven wrong, Ernie would have a night out at Varmer's expense. Ernie knew his horses far better than he knew his folk. He accepted the bet and won.

Varmer was a man of honour. Ernie was forced into his best suit and was wined and dined at the George and Pilgrim (where all the posh folk went). There were other pubs in Glastonbury, because it then had a population of about 5000. There was the Railway Inn, the Mitre Inn, British Legion, Rose and Crown, the Monarch, the Rifleman's Arms, the Constitutional, Queen's Head, the Glastonbury Arms, Waggon and Horses, First and Last, the Tap, Lamb Hotel, King William, Crown Hotel, Market House, and the Globe.

Ernie would have preferred any of these others, which was the reason why he was in the George and Pilgrim up to his neck in fine airs and good behaviour. They had a chicken dinner, and it wasn't Christmas. The wine flowed freely. ('Have some more wine, Ernie. There can't be a lot to it if the rich folk drink it.') From there they went to the Street Inn in Street, where an endless supply of whisky and cider was lavished upon the now bemused Ernie. He shakily sloped-off before closing time whilst Varmer remained to round the evening off. Being the perfect host, Varmer traced the staggered steps of Ernie and found him flat on his back two fields from home.

Varmer grabbed a limp leg under each arm and proceeded to *push* Ernie homewards! 'Ah', he once related to me, 'that stiff collar of Ernie's ploughed the straightest furrow you've ever seen.'

This, then, was the man who had decided to give Vather some special attention. He invited them all back to his barn where he kept enough cider to keep them senseless for the rest of their lives. A couple of very quick jars and then came the bait. With a few untrue boasts for some non-existent past topers of fame, he cast his line—'24 pints at one sitting!' (Vather could do that) . . . but Varmer Blaker hadn't finished. 'Sitting astride of a twenty gallon barrel' . . . (And Vather could do that) . . . 'Swigging from a half-gallon stone jar with no handle' . . . (He could do that too!) . . . 'Without getting off' . . . (And that!) . . . 'Refilling the jar himself, from the barrel he was sitting on' . . . (And that, as well!).

To straddle a twenty gallon barrel can be a painful experience to a non-equestrian. Varmer selected the barrel—one of his fine, old, farm-house-rough blends. It had been mutton-fed (raw mutton is placed in

the cider whilst it is maturing, and it picks the bones clean), and it had
the kick of Old Smarto's cart-horse with every swallow. Poor old Vather
was in up to his neck without even getting his feet wet. He was assisted
onto his unsaddled barrel. ('Hey! No need to push I down like that!–
Trying to split me difference?') The half-gallon stone jar was handed to
him. The contest commenced . . . and the old record still remains.

How had Vather got on? A sad shake of the head. 'He only finished
two jars.' Ah yes, but he'd been primed out-in-field, hadn't he?–Then
there were the two starting-drinks. Then another eight pints of special.
That wasn't too bad, really, not if you can get up after that lot, is it?
Another sad shake of the head. 'He *fell off* trying to fill the third jar.
Got up off the straw cussing and swearing–wanting to fight with everybody. I grabbed hold of him by the scroff and chucked him out on the
mangle-tip to sleep it off.' (That sounded like the Varmer I knew.)
'Summat must have upset him, I suppose,' I surmised. 'Summat had,'
he replied–'He said some bugger had pushed him!' (*That* sounded like
Vather.)

Swiggy Burrows . . . Somebody, somewhere, loved him I suppose. It
certainly wasn't anybody in our house! He was the apple of his mother's
eye. She lived in one of the stone houses across-road, and she was a
spasmodic sot (about once every night), and she'd give Vather a couple
of bob when he was broke, and press him with drink when she was
extra flush from the gee-gees. She didn't *like* doing these things, mind,
but she knew that it upset Our Mother. I wouldn't go as far as to say
that Our Mother and Gran hated one another's guts, because these views
were never aired in my presence, but I learnt to recognise the cold winds
of warning at a very early age, and it could have been the Ice Age.

Vather's father didn't live with Gran. He ran off to live over in Wales–
but it wasn't for 'nothing-bad'. He just wanted to get away from Our
Gran–proving he wasn't as 'dunch' as he was made out to be. He was
also said to be a drunken, bad-tempered, wife-beating bully, and, knowing Our Gran as I did, I'd say that that was another point in his favour. I
never met him and, on checking the family birth certificates, I find it
was a case of touch and go that Our Vather ever met up with him as
well.

Uncoo Awby, Vather's younger brother, lived with Gran and worked
hard at his studies to be as good as his 'older' brother. The only remain-
ing member of Gran's children was Aunt Ider, who lived next door with
Uncoo Taff. Aunt Ider's seven-stone, scrawny frame could not possibly
compete with the others, so she got 'drunker-quicker'–a sight more

often—on half as much.

With thirsts such as these, one could imagine an impending cider
drought, but it flowed on and on, at fivepence a quart. A quick, brief
spell of mental arithmetic will tell you that that makes it 'tuppence-hape-
me' a pint, and any self-respecting, cider-selling, landlord would inform
you he wouldn't dream of dealing in half measures. The two-handled
pint cider pot was well on its way in, though. Cider could also be
purchased more cheaply by the gallon or barrel from the local farms, so
it was often a case of going to the pub to get merry—to go home after
closing time to have a party.

Bunches of Bible Thumpers would attack the Beckery boundaries at
irregular intervals. There was one man of merit who delievered his best
sermons on the demon-drink when he was half-plastered. He never tried
to save Vather, thus conclusively proving to me that even the Good
Lord didn't want him. They preached the truth, mind. You know—'the
sins of the fathers upon the children'. I was thrown out of two Sunday
schools before I was nine years old. 'Suffer little children . . . ' Suffer . . .
Yes, I suffered. The Almighty was all powerful, but Our Mother could
run Him a close second when she came in swinging that boiler stick of
hers.

Going to School

One had to start going to school at the age of four in the old days of 1930. If you didn't *have* to, that was when most of the mothers would shove their 'little uns' off out of the way. Our Mother was no different, so off I had to go.

One can go to school on foot, on a bike, by car, by bus (on an egg, even), but have you ever been to school on the railings? The floods from the moor would come in past the Railway Station and cover the road and path. This meant we had to climb along the railings from the May Bush, and from there, up onto the top of Farmer Clark's wall to turn the corner until we came to dry land once more. This happened quite often in the winter, creating little or no problems to the horses and carts. Bicycles tended to adopt a collision course in the middle of the road, and I don't seem to remember any of the few privately owned motor cars attempting the crossing, but the lorry drivers seemed to hurl their lorries through to hurl the waves beneath our high and dry feet on the railings.

I could lace up my boots before I was old enough to go to school, but always had difficulty with the tying up. Our Mother did for me, while I stood with my piece of bread and dripping in my hand. This was breakfast, and would have to last me until dinner time. There were times when Mother had to put my leggings on for me, too. These 'leggins' were made of a thin 'mack' material with elastic at the top above the knee and another piece of 'laskit' to go under the instep of the boot. There was also 'hunderds' of little knob-buttons to do-up down the outsides. Under my overcoat I wore a jersey, and these usually had ties to match the colour and pattern on the collar. Everyone used to wear a jersey, and it was usual to appear without the tie after the first week. Grey flannel shirts were 'in'. We wore 'bracers' to keep our trousers up, and if one was lucky, one could also have a striped canvas belt which fastened up with a bent snake. The trousers were usually made of 'cordroy', grey flannel, or blue serge, and with the knee length stockings, hand knitted or bought, which always refused to stay up with or without the aid of garters, one could be said to be ready for the weather.

—Not a bit of it! You see, there was a space between the bottom of your trousers and those leggings, and those trousers had no button-up flies like the 'grow'd ups'. No. We just had a little peep-hole in our'n. Well, now . . . (don't think I'm being rude, telling you this, mind), but if you wanted to 'go' and you used that peep-hole, it meant having to move your shirt from the tucked-in position, which could prove to be 'a bit on the cold side'—so we used to use the trouser leg and come up under the shirt. You then 'went' down through the trouser leg. This was a good 'idear' from the cold weather preventions point of view, but created another problem . . . or two. As the old folk will tell you, 'Summers were hotter, winters were colder'—and we kids had the coldest hands in the world! This probably accounted for the reason we all adopted the same stance whilst 'going' . . . Head down, rounded shoulders, and tip-toe on the trouser leg-side that happened to be in use, to the accompaniment of strangled, stifled grunts.

There was something else. If that trouser leg happened to be a little on the tight side, the thigh between the legging and the bottom of the trouser leg was apt to get a little on the damp side. A quick wipe with the sleeve of your jersey was not the answer because the cold wind would play upon the slight salt deposit and we would finish up with a 'touch of the spree'. It was so sore. Most of us had ambidextrous legs, due to the fact that the choice usually depended on the warmest hand at the time, so we eventually ended up with a brace of sore legs. We would then run about like little jockies who had lost their horses. Our Mother used to put margarine or zinc ointment on it for me.

I well remember my first day at school. Saint Benedict's, it was called. There was a church with the same name just across the road, too.

'Miss' was there to look after us, and she sat me with Tubb and Ticker on their first day, as well. It was nice to meet someone in the same situation, and all three of us had a 'blimmin' good roar'. 'Miss' dried our tears and gave us some toys to play with.

After a while, we decided we wanted to 'go', but were afraid to ask in front of the other children, and decided to hang on "til come playtime'. A sad mistake, though, because the lavatories were behind the school at the far end of the playground, and Ticker and I couldn't make it. 'Where 'ere you be, let your . . .' goes the old country saying, and we did just that in a corner of the very busy front yard. Someone must have told on us, because 'Miss' arrived before we had finished and we, in a state of confused modesty, hurriedly cut short some half finished business with disastrous results.

Well, there you are. In trouble—first day at school, and Our Mother said she wasn't a bit surprised.

There were other days in the classroom when I would sit in my little round-backed chair and survey my surroundings. It was a typical Victorian affair. A very high ceiling with wooden beams. 'Like inside a church', I used to think. There was a heavy green-studded door with a ring-handle and latch and a big stone fireplace with a text carved into it. A stove had been placed in front of the fireplace and was fed with scuttle after scuttleful of coke. It was either too cold or too hot. Sometimes it used to glow red from halfway up and at the base of the pipe stack. Both stove and fireplace was enclosed with a high railed fireguard. The poker was nothing like the one we had at home, and consisted of a six-foot length of metal piping which 'Miss' would ram down into the stove through a little hinged door on the side of the top. The windows were as tall as church windows, and the bottom of them was too high up for a grown-up to look through. Cords were attached to the upper hinged casements to facilitate the opening and closing of them, but seldom worked due to the twists, tangles and knots.

Crates of bottles of milk was sometimes placed on the stove. One third of a pint, the bottles were. A bottle a day cost twopence-halfpenny a week. If you were thin and undernourished the Council paid. This made me a sort of Joe Muggins. I couldn't afford to buy it, and I was too healthy to get it for nothing. I quickly made friends with Norm, who was supplied with two free bottles a day and hated the taste of milk. He was thin. He was thin compared with the other thin kids, and with my help he remained that way to the end of his school days.

School bags hung on the walls containing books and rulers, etc., and each bag had coloured spots stuck on its outside like dice to teach us to count. I had no difficulty here, because we played whist and solo quite a lot at home. Our slates had wooden frames around them, and these were always placed under the long tables before going home. We sat both sides of these tables.

At the inner end of the classroom was a huge folding screen, consisting of wooden panels on the lower half and glass on the upper part. There was a door fitted into it, and even when this was closed I could hear what was going on in the other classroom with very little effort on my part. There was another 'Miss' in there, and she sounded a right old madam to me! She didn't half used to give them summat to be getting on with, I can tell you. She never stopped shouting . . .

'I told you to pay attention, didn't I?' . . . Bump, bump, bump!

'Keep quiet!' . . . Thump, thump, thump!

'Come out here at once!' . . . Bump, bump . . . (missed) . . . Bump!

I tell you, I didn't say anything at the time, but I hoped I would never be old enough to go up to Class II.

I shall not spend a lot of time relating my woes in the realms of Class II, because it was every bit as bad as I expected it to be.

'Miss' . . . (Sorry) . . . 'Madam' was a gaunt, thin woman in her late forties (this being a guess, as she never confided in me). Her black hair, streaked with grey, was drawn back into a severe bun, and odd bristly ends seemed to stick out from the back of her neck. She had black, fierce, staring eyes set in red veined, yellowish-whites, a long thin nose with a bulbous end, and a thin, waspish mouth which seemed to foam at the sides. Her complexion of red, black, and blue mottled hues altered rapidly according to the state of her temper.

She had a goitre in her throat.

She had no favourites. She hated all children.

She frightened every child to death, except me.

I wasn't afraid of her—I was terrified!

I 'drew' a bird sitting on a window sill. I used the ruled lines on the paper to enable me to form the window panes and the brickwork. She praised me in front of the class . . . and I had three hidings before I left school to go home that evening.

After prayers each morning, we had to show our hankies. We didn't have these in our house. We used our jersey sleeves, and we had the shiny patches to prove it, too. But 'Madam' said we *had* to have a hanky! Our Mother used to tear up pieces of rag, but we lost them. The safety-pin to the front of the jersey didn't work, either. We tore our jersies. 'I can't keep on tearing up rags for hankies,' Mother would say. And she was right. She couldn't. We were wearing them!

I had a decent bit of soft sheet one day. I was going to look after that 'all week', I decided, and put it in a safe place. Just before we entered the classroom I discovered I had lost it, and I *had* to have a hanky! A bit of quick thinking and I came up with the solution. I went through all the pockets of the overcoats hanging in the cloakroom and struck gold.

We said prayers. We held up our hankies. There I stood, without a care in the world . . . for a while . . . and something seemed to be going wrong. 'Madam' was scowling in my direction, and seemed to be encouraging the rest of the class to follow suit.

'Come out!' she thundered, and I obeyed. The Gestapo was unheard of, then, but I knew all about the third degree which the American police gave to the robbers, and I can assure you it was hell, even without the bright light shining in my eyes. 'Who's hanky is it?' . . . Mine . . . 'Where did you find it?' . . . I didn't, Miss . . . 'Why haven't you had a hanky like that before?' . . . Don't know, Miss . . . 'You stole it, didn't you?' . . . No, Miss . . . 'Why did you steal it?' . . . (Why?—because you'd knock the blimmin' hell out of me if I didn't have one!) . . . Don't know, Miss . . .

Well . . . I *had* to give in, didn't I? Something had gone wrong from the start. Somebody must have told on me.

'You (bump) lying, (bump) thieving, (bump) little (bump) toad!' (bump). I had to be punished for my crime and was dragged to the head mistress, who gave me a long lecture, punctuated by a 'Yes, Miss', 'No, Miss', or 'Sorry, Miss', every time she paused for a breath, and I still finished up with three on each hand!

Oh, the shame and humiliation. I had learn my lesson. The next time I stole a handkerchief, it wouldn't be a pink one—initialled—nor with a fancy lace border!—And it wasn't even big enough for a couple of good blows! Later on in the day I found my piece of rag in the folds of my left stocking. 'Just my luck,' I thought, 'I haven't even got a runny nose, now'. A little later, I had lost it again. It was taken away from me because I got caught making a sausage with it . . . Or was it a cracker? . . . Or . . . Pull one end and make a carrot?

We had those double desks with the pull-down seats which were fixed to a cast-iron frame holding the desk and the seats in one unit. 'Madam' made me sit next to the girl who wouldn't 'go'. Well, she 'went', but she didn't go to 'do it', if you see what I mean. Cooh! She used to smell terrible, but who was I to complain? There was that 'other day'. I had a bad dose of the backdoor trot—you know, the 'runs' (too many green apples, I expect). 'She'll love me for this,' I thought.

'Please Miss, can I leave the room?'

'Can't you wait until playtime?'

'No, Miss—Oops! No, Miss, I can't.'

She let me go the first time. She shrieked herself to within half an inch of a nervous breakdown on the second time of asking, and I only just made it. The third time, ten minutes later, was just too much for her. No, I couldn't go. No, and that was her last word on the subject . . . and I had to be sent home—holding tightly to the screwed up bottoms of my trouser legs because I had on a pair of clean stockings.

'We only remember the good times', they say.
This is all I remember of Class II.
My elder brother remembers nothing.

Merry England

Glastonbury had her legends and heroes. There was Abbot Whiting, King Arthur (and the Knights of the Round Table, I suppose,) but we of Beckery had our own protector. I never saw him mounted on a white horse, nor any other horse for that matter, but he rode high amongst us. He loved kids, especially the Beckery kids. We looked upon him as our own Saint George and he seemed to revel in slaying the many of our would-be dragons.

A tallish man, he was, and the sheer girth of his body made him look shorter. He was built and shaped like an oak cask and about ten times as strong. The hoop-iron bands were missing, of course, and these were replaced with the one broad leather belt which seemed to hang from his back-trouser buttons down to the big, square, brass buckle that nestled somewhere between his stomach and his navel. His 'bracers' suspended his brown 'cordroy' trousers, and he usually wore 'yarks' tied below each knee to keep the bottoms clear of the mud and hobnail boots. His breastplate was a 'weskit' that seldom buttoned up like any other waist-coat, and his collarless, striped, flannel shirts had permanently rolled-up sleeves which were never seen to cover the forearms of genuine Somerset mahogany. He never wore mailed gauntlets, or gloves—they didn't make them that big!

His face was etched with the years of working outdoors, for he was a craftsman when it came to hedging, ditching, or fencing. The big, droopy, walrus moustache tended to soften the broad, hawk-like nose and the equally hawk-like eyes of pale blue. His helmet was the shameless, shape-less remains of a felt trilby of which the rim had long since passed from recognition and had joined the shape of the crown to cover his bristly, grey-black hair like a soft pudding basin. And there, with a plume of blue-grey smoke from his stubbed-clay of Black Bell Shag, you have our champion, Old Regg'o England.

His trade necessitated quite an armoury of tools. There was the open-sectioned box with the hoop-iron handle, containing nails, staples, pincers, and a hammer. There was also the sack bag containing a reap hook, staff hook, bill hook, axe, and another long-handled, straight-

18

bladed implement which he called his 'slasher'. A keen edge was kept on
these tools with frequent 'chew-wit—chew-wits' of the 'bawker' (whet-
stone), which he carried in a 'budget' (sheath), attached to his waist.
Each tool was individually wrapped in oiled sacking to prevent 'rusting
and contact with the other.

On certain occasions we were allowed to help 'carr' the kit, and he
would then give us the dubious honour of carrying his mallet. This was
no ordinary mallet for it had a head of solid hardwood shaped like a
five gallon barrel about 15-16 inches in diameter, and bound with hoop-
iron.

'No openin' no gates, and no draggin' neither,' would be the order of
the day, and he would roar with laughter at the antics of three small
children attempting to manhandle their clumsy load—one each side of
the head—bent almost double, and inching along with faltering side-
scuffs whilst the lucky third held the end of the handle and pretended
to suffer.

The mallet was too large to pass through or under the gates.

'Aw, Mister England, can't we just open this one?'

'No. No openin'. That's the rules, see?' . . . and over the gate it
would have to go.

'Mind you don't drop him, me dears . . . Don't want to break him,
do we? Haw, Haw.' There was always this eternal struggle to 'hix', or
hook the head of the mallet onto the top rail.

'That's right, me dears. All together, heft! And none of that swearin',
mind. Save your breath for the next one'.

'Hix un on the top first, like Mister England said. Lift a bit higher
up, will 'ee?'

'No, not the handle, Dafty! T'other end!'

'I'll get up-top and hold un.'

'No I'll do that. You can do the next gate.'

'*I'll* do it. You only carr'd the handle!'

'Now come on, me dears. No arggin 'tween the three of 'ee . . . You've
got to work friendly together . . . "More the hands, lighter the work," so
they say . . . Lovely, lovely. That's lovely! Well done, me dears . . . Haw,
haw, haw . . . Well, come on then. This is no place to get "stooded" . . .
Come on, there's two more gates to go yet!'

We would arrive 'on site' completely exhausted, and then Old Regg'o
would commence work with the job in hand. We didn't interfere. Use of
the cutting tools was out of the question. Straining and cutting the wire,
and carrying the lopped branches to the fire was not allowed. ('T'were

too dange-rous.') This only left our friend the mallet, and for some
reason or another, we had never asked for a 'go' with that! Once, and
once only, he allowed us to hold a stake whilst he hammered it home.
Not as dangerous as you may think, because many small, argumentative
hands tend to wobble the stake all over the place, so a massive left hand
steadied our unsteadiness, and a right hand would lift the mallet with
ease to punch the stake into the ground so as to remove it beyond the
limitations of our misguided intentions. Even the light 'starting taps'
tended to drag the stake too savagely through our hands, and we were
cured after the one 'go'.

'Nunch-time' came about ten o'clock. Old Regg'o would sit upon his
mallet and we would gather around him. Everyone, no doubt, has tasted
bread, cheese, and raw onion—but have you ever tasted bread, cheese,
and raw onion that has been wrapped in a red handkerchief?—There's
nothing like it! He would cut the onion into segments with his pocket
knife, and then, placing a large piece of cheese upon a quarter of a black-
crusted cottage loaf, he would cut a hunk of bread and cheese together,
add a piece of onion, and then with the knife blade, bread, cheese, and
onion sandwiched between thumb and forefinger, it would be delivered
into our greedy hands. Just like a picnic? No. We had earnt this, so it
was 'work food' with a taste beyond the wildest dreams—more like an
outdoor banquet, I'd say.

Old Regg'o wasn't always with us. He couldn't go to school with us,
for instance.

A hole in the ground is just a hole in the ground until that hole is placed
in a road with a man stood in it, and then folk will be *drawn* to it like a
magnet. I was no exception, and you can imagine my delight when, after
a hard day's work at school, I espied these two holes in the pavement
with two men standing in one of them. The holes were about ten yards
apart. I eyed up the situation with a critical eye, and the two men eyed
me with suspicious, self-rightous scowls of condemnation that could be
hurtful at times. The empty hole came first. At the bottom were the
ends of two small-bore metal pipes, and things looked similar in the
workmen's hole. 'Must be some sort of trouble with the pipes,' I surmised.

The work did not proceed, and I sensed the atmosphere that usually
preceeds a, 'Hoy, Young Swiggy!—Hike it!' Yes, we had met before, and
they remembered me only too clearly from my escapades of the last
year or so. I could see I would have to lay on a bit of the old charm here.

'Howdy do?' I cheerfully said. They didn't reply, and I remained in a lonely vacuum of an imminent thunderstorm. Why did they treat me so? After all, I wasn't standing on their slippery pile of precious rubble this time, was I? (And the other time?) Well, yes, I *had* kicked that stone down into the trench—but only to see it splash into the water at the bottom. I didn't know he was going to bend his head in the way, did I? (And the red lamp?) What lamp? Oh, the red light . . . Well, that crook'd handle on the top of it caught in my stocking, didn't it—It wouldn't have happened if my stockings would stay up! Why *me* all the time, anyroad? (And the tea bottle?) Look. I didn't break that. I wasn't the only one throwing stones, was I?—And, *WHO* throw'd snowballs at me? I called one of the workmen 'Snowball' because he threw an ice-hard snowball at me which just about knocked me sick. I made light of it at the time and laughed with them, but later retired behind the Police Station wall to have a good cry in privacy.

Still no sign of a thaw in their friendless faces. Unknown to me, they had a form of a pump in use. They would pump it up to compress the air and, after placing the nozzle at one end of the pipe, they would release the air to blast the dust or rust out of the other end.

'Go down t'other hole and fetch I me spanner,' Snowball commanded. I was astounded. No abuse. I was not being 'hiked' on, and I was not only being allowed to watch, but was being asked to help, as well! I walked on air to the other hole. I let them down, of course. (The shame of it!)—My first official act in the noble art of hole-making and I couldn't see any spanner. 'Look down by the pipes, then,' they told me, and I did.

I seem to recall a sort of half-hearted puff of blue, red and black cloud of pain. I couldn't see! I cried, and they laughed. I cried louder.

'What's the matter with all that noise, me son?'

'They've blow'd stuff in me eyes,' I answered.

'But you shouldn't be down in that hole in the first place, should 'ee?'

'They told me to get the spanner, Mister England.'

'Here, blow your nose in this,' and I was handed a handkerchief. I blew. I could hear their voices.

'We only done it for a laugh, Reg.'

'I know. And didn't I hear thee laughin' at a little young'un cryin'?' BUMP!

'T'were only a joke, Reg.'

'We all like jokes. Now we'll all have one—just between we!'

THUMP! There followed the sound of a scuffle. I dabbed my eyes and managed to get a bleary view of Old Regg'o holding someone at arms' length with his left hand, whilst he belted him with the right. I dabbed my eyes again. Snowball was up to his neck in his waist-deep hole, feebly prodding the rim with his elbows in an attempt to remove his right knee from under his chin which tended to tilt his face skyward. Regg'o paused in mid-thump to study Snowball's progress, whilst the other man patiently waited like an empty sack at the far end of Regg'o's arm. With a long groan Snowball gave up the ghost and returned to the prone position. Regg'o then eyed the inert form in his hand, and gently lowered him onto the pile of rubble.

I had another good blow into the handkerchief. It was a red one, better than the bits of rag I was used to.

'Better let I have me "hankacher" back now,' he said, and I complied.

'Thanks, Mister England.'

'Cooh!' he exclaimed. 'When were the last time you blow'd your nose?—Christmas? You better let your mother wash un, and then let I have it back. Can't wrap me lunch in a hankacher like that, I can't.'

'Right'o, Mister England.'

I wondered if he'd mind if I left it a day or two, to enable me to blow my nose in front of the other school kids with their bits of rag and shiny jersey sleeves. A heavy hand covered the width of my shoulders.

'Come on, me son. Let's go on down home.'

So, off-down-home, we went.

'Saint George and Merry England!'

The next time you hear this battle cry, you will then realize who the other bloke is, won't you?

Those Who Came

Beckery, in its isolation, had lots of callers in the form of trades-folk.

The postman wore a sloping-back hat like a fireman's helmet which didn't shine.

The oilman came around with his lorry loaded high with anything from a spare crock to a coconut mat. Kiddles (or a kettle, if you wish), cups, saucers, plates, clothes pegs, basticks (or baskets), bastick chairs, and brooms to sell to the folk. And, of course, the oil was paraffin.

There were two different milkmen. They would both arrive by pony and float, with a step-up at the back to get in, and they both had a gert, shiny churn up-front with a brass tap at the bottom. They sold their milk from smaller cans which they would carry from door to door and measure it out into m'lady's jugs.

Our baker had a pony and trap, and the trap was covered in like a small caravan with an open front. It also had a small backdoor, and I once hung onto the backdoor to keep pace with the fleet-footed pony. I must have twisted the handle because I finished up with loaves all over the road, and it was at this point that I started to leave the pony behind. The baker would leave our bread inside the door on the foot of the stairs, where we would remove the middle of the loaves bit by bit while it was still warm. This annoyed Vather because his haunches (hunks) of cheese would fall through his slices of bread (or so he told us). The shelves inside the baker's cart were covered with close-woven flour sacks and each day he would shake them out and put the crust crumbs into a paper bag. These were given to the children (except me), and were eaten like sweets.

Old Missiz Jones from the moor, came once a week to sell her 'turfs'—peat, cut in square biscuits. She had a pony and float, but there was no step at the back because she always had the tailboard up to prevent the turfs from falling out. (And to keep down the draught, as she once told me.) The turfs cost a tanner (sixpence), a big basketful. Folk used them to light their fires.

Then there was Mister Chiffers, the fish bloke. He had a very small pony. I can't say what the cart was. It looked like a little box on two

wheels. (I think it was home-made.) He would open the back of the
little cart, and down would come the tailboard with the chopping block
attached. Out would come the scales, me lads. There were shelves around
the inside. It was like a little shop in there! I started going the rounds
with him on Saturday mornings when I was about seven years old, and
my job was to run from door to door with the plates and the change.
Mister Chiffers had a very loud husky voice. He spoke with a bellow.

'Ring the bell, Bwoy!—I'll do the shoutin'!'

I would then grab the big brass hand bell . . . climb down from the
cart (because I didn't used to like the way the pony flattened his ears
when I rang it) . . . move to the side of the pony (remembering 'Haven't
never know'd a cow or a hoss what could kick sideways, yet!) . . . and
ring the bell. What a noise! Marvellous, it was. My spell of duty would
last from about half-past seven to about half-past one. Mister Chiffers
would give me a tanner and enough fish for dinner for the family.

The tanner paid for the turf.

Mister Chiffers was a very fair and understanding man.

Mister Crees came around in a big old van to sell green grocery and
rabbits.

Our Gramf would call at our house with his S & D. J.R. horse and
cart for a cup of tea. A very quiet cart-horse, Gramf had. 'Biggest and
the bestest cart horse you'll ever find.' Our Gramf told me that.

The sawmill horses came up through sometimes. Three cart-horses
linked together pulling a log waggon, which looked like a big square
pole on two pairs of wheels. 'No horse worked harder than they did'. Our
Gramf said that, as well.

There was another baker, Mister Wadman. A very tiny little man,
pale faced with a square black moustache. He always wore a dark grey
suit and a large bowler hat . . . Or was it a *large* bowler hat? It *was* a bowler
hat . . . It looked large on him, though. He pushed a red, heavy, two-
wheeled barrow, and you couldn't see the top of his bowler when he
was on the move—head down—pushing. He lived right at the top of
town, and that's a long way up—especially with that barrow. All the
way down to our place just to sell a couple of loaves, and then it was
off back to the top of town again to start baking for tomorrow. Yes, a
very tiny man, he was—big for his size though!

The big black steam lorry from the town Gas Works used to stop
halfway down the road when Mister Snooks wanted a cup of tea. Mr
Snooks, the driver, was also a fireman and we would sometimes see him
rush home, put his clothes and brass helmet on, and then rush off up

the road on his bike. Judging by the speech and the smoke that used to pour out of that lorry of his, I think he *had* to be a fireman to be able to drive it! Still, as he always said, 'Haven't never had no puncture, yet.' Shouldn't think he had. That steam lorry had solid tyres.

Mister Sweet, the insurance man, always wore his best blue suit when he did his rounds on his bike.

Mister Oods (Woods) would walk down from the factory wearing his steel-rimmed clogs, and with sacking wrapped around his knees and shins. I saw him wearing a red rubber apron once, as well.

Mister Champion brought the coal by horse and waggon—a flat-bedded waggon, it was.

'A bag of Derby nuts, please,' Mother would shout, 'and not so much steam coal in with it this time, neither!'

They'd have a few more words about this while he collected the money, he declaring his innocence, and Our Mother knowing steam coal when she saw it. They were both right, because we had stolen the steam coal from the factory, and we weren't allowed to steal, so we said nothing.

Feeding Time

This was always the best time of the day for me. I have always liked my food.

Breakfast was usually a piece of bread and dripping, bread and lard, or bread and jam—plum jam. No one seemed to be able to make any other kind. On Sunday mornings we could have fried bread and egg, or fried bread and bacon, and on some Sunday mornings there was just fried bread. (Too much fried food wasn't no good for you, anyroad.)

There was usually the one cooked meal each day at dinner time (Noon). We would have a joint of roast lamb most Sundays, and a little less, warmed up on Mondays. The other weekday dinners would consist mostly of stews, or greens, potatoes and egg, greens, potatoes and bacon, or greens and potatoes with thick flowery gravy.

Teatime was a spaced-out affair because we usually took our slice of bread and summat and rushed out to play. Now and again a half-pound bag of biscuits would be bought from the local shop and these were religiously shared out equally. I used to like to keep mine until I went out to play so that I could show off to the other less fortunate kids. As we got older, we would have a cup of cocoa and bread and cheese at supper time.

It was no good going into our house at meal times expecting to get your meal straightaway. We were a large family and there was always a shortage of space, cutlery, and cups—with and without handles.

I had my favourite meals. Rabbit stew—there's nothing like it! All done thick with potatoes and doughboys, and plenty of liquid to soak up with your bread. We all had our favourite parts of the rabbit. I liked the rib cage, and could do a beautiful job of nibbling those bones clean. Vather liked the head 'because the brains did him good' (better than nothing, I suppose). Vather either had, or didn't have false teeth, so he used to get one of us to bite the skull open for him. I was quite good at this, but lost the job when a rabbit arrived with less brain than Vather, and he thought the worst of everyone.

Pea soup. Glory, Glory! The dried marrowfat peas had to be soaked overnight with a lump of baking soda in the water. We would help ourselves from the huge iron saucepan on the hob. Marrow bones, meat scraps, potatoes and doughboys. This was a meal for a king. It was so thick, the ladle would have stood up in the middle unassisted, but we didn't have one of those, and used a cup with a handle instead. After using it, you replaced it on a plate beside the saucepan and if you didn't like the next one in the queue behind you—you dropped it into the saucepan and smiled as you apologised.

Chester cake—bread pudding with mixed spice and currants 'in' and no pastry 'on'. Mother put lots of suet into it to make it nice and fatty. It was made three inches thick in a full-size oven dish, and we used to squabble for the four corner pieces which had been more burnt than the rest. The currants on the surface used to come out of the oven like hollow charcoal marbles. Delectable!

Spotted Dick, a big suet pudding with sultanas and currants, tied up in a cloth and boiled in the iron saucepan. Eaten hot, with a thick layer of jam on it. We liked them on the heavy side. None of that hairy-fairy stuff for us. You know what I mean—it would stick to both sides of your spoon—like doughboys! I think Mother was glad we appreciated them like this, because I don't think she could make them any other way. And if you think that's a good laugh, you ought to try her cakes! The only time they would rise was when we assisted them to our mouths. Give Mother her due, mind. Nothing was ever left over.

Faggots. There is no one who can make faggots like Our Mother. She would make the mixture of liver, lites, bacon fat, sage, onions and stale bread and mould the faggots into cricket-sized balls. These were then covered with 'caul', 'ketchin', or 'ketcher', and baked in the bread-pudding dish. They would have melted in the mouth had we given them the time.

Now and again we would get pigs trotters, chiddlings or chitterlings, tripe and onions, baked cheese and onions.

This mouth-watering list must make one think that our house was a house of plenty. It wasn't. We had our hard times, as well. I can remember coming home to a cooked dinner of Quaker Oats with no sugar. We went hungry at times, but we were never starving. We were lucky.

I remember the time when there was nothing but the one scrawny chicken running about in the backyard, and us with no coal or wood to burn in the fireplace, and no money for the gas. We were sent out to collect scrap iron, which we did, and returned home triumphantly with the huge sum of fourpence. This incident sticks in my mind very clearly, because someone left their good lorry beside some old scrap lorries in the timber yard, and it received the same treatment as the others when we descended upon them like a plague of locusts armed with a pair of broken cobbler's pincers.

The first three of us had a 'touch of rickets', so we would go with Vather to collect snails. The snails on walls or stones were safe, but the snails on greenstuff were poisonous—so 'they' said. These were boiled three times in brine, and then we would sit and eat them like huge winkles, 'hoking' them out of their shells with a darning needle. They were delicious. Vather preferred them to pickled onions with his bread and cheese.

There was the time when he forgot to replace the lid of the saucepan for the first boil, and when Mother went out into the backhouse (scullery) there were snails all over the oven, on the floor, on the doors and windows, up on the walls and the ceiling. It didn't take us too long to catch them again, because they don't move very fast—even with salt on their tails.

We had chicken for dinner every Christmas. Very nice, too. I enjoyed it, but not nearly as much as I enjoyed the bread and chicken dripping in the evening, when we would sit and listen to the wireless after the young'uns had gone to bed.

All a matter of taste, I suppose.

What's in a Name

Funny things, names. Folk are born with a name and sometimes
christened with another, and this gives one an official and personal form
of recognition for the rest of one's life.

Were the names in our community of a more possessive nature, I
wonder?

We didn't stop with naming folk. Animals and objects had their
special names, and domesticated animals were given the surnames of
their family to boot. Here are some of the dogs I remember.

Tacks Burrows: A good natured Airedale bitch with a savage hate for
strangers and trespassers. Loved children, rabbiting and
ratting.

Rags Robins: A liver and white Cocker Spaniel who had mad spates
of worm-worry and dragged a one-foot bare patch off
the bottoms of all the hedges down our road. His
owners and I were the only friends he had.

Rover Dennis: A large black and white cow dog type, who would
hide inside his own front gate to pounce on the unsuspecting. Not a very fierce dog—if one remembered
to step off the pavement whilst passing *his* house.

Rock Badman: A gold and white, smooth-haired, terrier-beagle cross.
He loved children and hated grown-ups. He was a
roamer, but would never go into the town. He would
go on hunting trips for days on end and, should our
paths cross, he would sort of encourage us to join him.
I tended to regard him as a thinking-type dog.

Tine Pugh: She was far from tiny, but a first-class ratter for all
that. She was fat and overfed and protected the source
of her next meal like a 'good un'.

Spot Snooks: A snappy Jack Russell. A first class ratter, but seldom
seen off the lead. (Waste of a good dog, we thought.)

Fido Wall: He was the smallest dog down our road, and his mongrel
varieties had Heinz's 57 beaten by miles. He didn't
growl, snap, snarl, rat, or hunt, and acted like the

world's biggest coward, and was the apple of his boss's
eye. A nice little dog, even though he was a little short-
sighted. I once saw him scent a stationary elephant at
the circus. He got closer and closer, nose sniffing the
air, and when the elephant moved poor old Fido kye-
eyed a non-stop trail to home where he remained
under the sofa until his boss came home.

The cats had surnames, too, but tended to be less important than
dogs.

Tabbs Burrows:	Not a very imaginative name.
Pete Dennis:	A large black and white who ate more meat in a day than I did in a week. He had his front leg cut off by the horse-drawn mowing machine.
Tibby Pugh:	A useless long-haired, brown-black cat. She suffered the same fate as the bitch, Tine, and was overfed and spoilt.

Then there were the names for 'things'. There were hundreds of elm
trees around our area, but the tree on the opposite side of the road from
us was called 'The Elum'. There were hundreds of hawthorn bushes, as
well, and the one that grew beside our road not far from the sawmill
was called 'Maybush'.

Our lamp posts weren't just ordinary gas lamps. They were special.

Bridge Lamp:	The lamp on the bridge above Baily's.
Mill Lamp:	The lamp at the entrance of the Mill Lane.
Snook's Lamp:	The lamp outside the Snook's residence.
New Lamp:	The lamp at the junction with the New Road.
Middle Lamp:	The lamp midway between Beckery and the railway junction.
Maybush Lamp:	The lamp beside the Maybush.
Station Lamp:	The lamp in the middle of the road at the railway junction.

Our's—our'n. 'Our house'. 'That road of our'n.' 'Our Young'un',
which can refer to my elder brother as well as the younger ones. 'Alright,
Young'un?' can be used as a friendly greeting to someone older or
younger who is not a member of the family. Within the 'fambly' the

governing factor is 'of us'. Ron'us. Ray'us. Tone'us. Pete'us. Val'us. Dave'us. Mike'us. Bade'us. (That was the list of our family—not counting Our Mother and Our Vather.)

Then come the friends of our'n, or members of our community. Regg'o. Jack'o. Bill'o. Herb'o. John'o. Ted'o. Ed'o.

To call an old man 'old' can be an insult, but to refer to him as 'Old Un' is a mark of respect to his old age. 'Poor old Chols' could be the same age, or younger than the speaker when this is spoken with pity or affection.

The mystery of the nicknames come next, and I am so glad to think someone started this habit. There are the usual everyday ones. Dusty Miller. Jumper Cross. Snowy White. Leafy Green. Jock. Paddy. Taff. Some referred to the person's physical appearance. Tiny, or Mousey, Lofty, Tubby—and Daylight Simms had bowed-legs. As I have already informed you, Vather's nickname was Swiggy. His children became known as 'Young Swiggy' by their elders, and 'Swiggy' by the other children of their own age. This can prove difficult at times when there are so many children in one family, so it isn't long before the non-family folk find another name for each individual—and with no help from the person concerned.

Burrows . . . Rabbits' burrows . . . Bunny Burrows. This nickname lasts only for a while because it is too general for a lot of brothers, so the change starts again. My elder brother is known as Admiral. He was in the Navy and his father's name was Nelson. I always call him Cudge— I don't know why. I was in the Navy. *My* father's name was Nelson, and I was never called Admiral. Things took a different path. Bunny Burrows . . . Bunny Rabbit . . . Bugs Bunny . . . I grew a beard . . . Bug-whiskered . . . Bugs Burrows . . . Bugsy, to others. I have looked this up in the dictionary: 'Flat, ill-smelling, blood-sucking insect, infesting beds'. (Flattering devils!)

I will answer to the name of 'Ray' to anyone, prepared to accept whatever comes. When addressed as 'Raymond' as a child, this usually came as a prelude to a reprimand, and I dislike that name even to this day. When referred to as 'Bugs' I can always be sure I am being addressed by a friend who knows me well, or by someone who wants to know me better.

I shall now give you a detailed view on a couple of folk who earnt nicknames to suit their characters.

I shall tell you of Dobbin, and before you start guessing—don't! Dob-

bin was a bloke—not a horse. An old-fashioned cup of tea, he was. He
was obliging. He was willing. He was eager to please others. He would
do anything for anyone, and would 'go-at-it' like a bull at a gate whilst
doing so. He could never go slow.

Our Gramf once said of him, 'Give him a kind word and a pat on the
head, and he'll go all day,' and added, 'If ever Oliver (his horse) do get
bad, I don't think I can do worse than to hitch Dobbin in the shafts.'
Remembering this, I later studied Dobbin's great big square chin and
realized that Gramf was right. A nosebag on that chin would never look
out of place. He was about five-foot-six, and must have 'hurned out' (or
runned out) at about fourteen stone. He had red hair, a red face, and
little beady blue eyes above the pug nose. The big ham-chin matched the
two hams on the ends of his arms. I had never seen such gert hands! He
wore farm clothing, and worked on a farm out-in moor.

His real name was Robin. Can you imagine a bloke like this with a
name like that? So we called him Dobbin.

One always knew when Dobbin was about—even when he happened
to be out of sight. He was the noisiest, clumsiest person for miles around,
and he could talk to you from the other end of the road, whereas he
would not hear your shouted replies. His shouts could be heard from the
top of Weary All to the Railway Station with the wind against him. He
would sing songs as he worked to his own untuneful tunes, using his
own instant-composed, meaningless lyrics:

> Please run up the mountain, dear.
> I'll be up-top perty soon.
> Flies and bees don't bother I.
> Tis a hot time now, for June.

That was one of his better ones.

He was sharp and witty, and was never found wanting for an answer.
Shooting and hunting was his life-long hobby, and he was sharp and
efficient at this, too. Vather once said, 'If you get drunk during the duck
season, don't fall in the rhine,* 'cos Dobbin would have you before the
splash had settled.' And Vather should know, because he often fell in the
rhine.

Dobbin loved to tell-up a tale. There were lots of old jokes one would
hear again and again. You know—

There were two men working in a field.

*rhine: pronounced 'reen'—drainage ditch.

One says to the other, 'Wind's blowin' up a bit.'
'Ah, there is a bit of a draught,' the other replied,
'Go down and shut thiick gate, will 'ee?'

Another. A town bloke in a car asked a farmer the way without saying 'please'.

'Where does this road lead to?'
'Dunno'.
'What is the place I have just passed through?'
'Dunno'.
'Don't know?—Are you daft or something?'
'Might be—but I ain't lost, be I?'

And another. A bloke up-top a hayrick, and the others take the ladder away.

'How do I get down now?' he asked.
'Close thy eyes and walk about a bit,' they reply.

And another. Farmer catches a town bloke in his orchard.

'What be you doin' here?' Farmer asked.
'Oh, just looking. Have you seen a waggon-load of monkeys pass by?'
'No, can't say I have. Why, have you falled off of one?

Do you see what I mean? They are all very old jokes.

Dobbin's yarns were different. They were new. He approached me with some rabbits over his shoulder . . .

'Do you want a rabbit for thy mother, Young'un?' he asked. 'Only a tanner if you let I have the skin back.'

'Ah, alright, Dobbin,' I said . . . (It hadn't been shot.) 'Snared?' I asked.

'No, not snared, me son . . . Netted. Went ferretin' yesterday . . . Ah . . . Varmer took I up over the hill to one of his friend's place . . . Caw, gert big place, t'were . . . None of thy rubbish there, there weren't . . . That's the kind of friends to have, s'no . . . Ahhh . . . I had to go catchin' rabbits on the lawn. LAWN? T'were bigger than any six fields I've seen 'round here! Ahhh . . . All posh, t'were . . . You know how tis, I had to give me ferrets a bath before I took them up there!'

Off he went,

I've been makin' hayricks.
I went and jumped a stile.
Tor Fair's here, and I don't care.
So darlin', don't thee smile.

A lovely song to hear—from about five miles away.

And did you ever hear-tell of Billy-go-deeper?

Billy lived two or three miles from here, and these things happened about fifty years ago, I expect. He has gone on, now. Died about ten years ago.

He kept a lot of horses for carrying stone from up on the Street Quarr' down to the village of Compton Dundon. The stone was blue lias, and was used for building houses and walls. (Before I commence this story I would like to remind you that folk in those days had to make their own kind of fun, and they didn't bide waiting around for someone to come along and tell them *how* to enjoy themselves.)

Billy would get up to more tricks than a waggon-load of monkeys—full of them, he was. He would always carry an empty matchbox about with him, and when he asked you for a match—look out! He would light his clay and then return his empty matchbox to you. He had a couple of blokes in there one day to kill a pig for him and, before they arrived at Billy's place, someone had warned them about the matchbox trick. They were very pleased to know about it, too, because it wasn't just Billy who liked his bit of fun.

'Got a match on thee, Billy?' one of them asked.

Billy, unsuspecting, handed his good matchbox to the man, who lit his pipe, and, keeping the full box inside his hand, offered an empty box to Billy. He shook his hand to rattle the matches, and Billy, with his mind on the pig, took the empty box and placed it in his weskit pocket. Those two blokes looked like a couple of dogs with ten tails a'piece who had just discovered where lamp posts were made. A little later Billy came into the shed again. He had his clay in his mouth and he was slapping his pockets.

'What's up, Billy?' one of them asked. 'Lost thy matches?'

'No,' said Billy. 'Must a'left me baccy in-house, I think.'

'Well, they *had* to see Billy use that empty matchbox, didn't they? One of them offered Billy a fill from his baccy-tin, adding with a grin, 'You don't mind if I keep-hold of it while you'm fillin' up, do 'ee?' Billy got his gert paws over the tin and commenced to fill his pipe. (It's a slow,

steady job to fill a clay with shag, you know.) The man pretended to
check his tin when Billy had finished and discovered that it was empty!

'Hey, Billy,' he exclaimed. 'How big is thiick pipe of your'n?'

'Same size as thine,' replied Billy, 'but I do always carry a little
extra summat up me sleeve!' And Billy showed him. That was where he
had stuffed the man's baccy!

'Billy,' said the baccy-bloke, 'you'm the blimmin' lick! I s'pose you
want I to give thee a match, as well?'

'Ah, you'd better,' replied Billy, 'that's if you don't want to chuck
up smokin' for the rest of the day.'

Billy did wear a beautiful silver half-hunter and double Albert on his
weskit. Every time he went to the market a farmer would come up to
him and shout so that others could hear,

'Sight—unseen. My gold watch for thine, Billy!' The farmer had been
doing this for years, and Billy had never been tempted,—until this particular day. He had hardly entered the market when,

'Sight—unseen. My gold watch for thine, Billy!'

'Well now,' said Billy, 'You've been hoopyin' and hollerin' about
thiick watch of thine long enough—I'm blowed if I don't take thee up
on it.' They spit and shook hands, which means a lot in front of witnesses. Farmer couldn't get his watch out of his pocket fast enough. He
looked the happiest bloke in the world with all those onlookers. He
turned the watch over and showed it to Billy.

'There you be,' he said. 'I ain't tellin' lies to thee. He's marked
"gold".' Billy examined it . . . 'Ah, he's gold alright, but he haven't got
no hands on un,' he pointed out.

'Hah!—And that ain't all of it!' Farmer retorted. 'He haven't got no
innards in un, neither! Come on Billy, sight—unseen!'

'That's true. You'm not wrong,' said Billy. He took his watch from
his pocket and looked at it with deep sorrow. Then he unhooked it
from the double Albert and handed it to his tormentor. Farmer grabbed
greedily at the watch as if it was the Fat Stock First Prize. He cupped
the watch in both hands and beamed at it, and then the smile dropped
from his chops a sight faster than the selling price when one is buying.

'Yer, hang on a minute!' he exclaimed. 'This watch ain't thy silver
hunter!'

'And do 'ee think I don't know that?' replied Billy. 'I left it home
today, 'cos I fancied I might bump into thee, as usual. Still . . . He *have*
got hands on, and he *do* go . . . Should do, he cost I a half-a-crown down

Tor Fair the other day . . . How much do 'ee think I can get for this
gold watch case?'

Farmer didn't say nothing.

There is also the story of the pears.

Billy had two pear trees just outside his backdoor. There aren't many
good pear trees around this area, but these were two of them. A shopkeeper from up town used to come to Billy to buy the pears in order
to re-sell them in his shop. He liked to buy them just right.

'Be the pears ripe?' he enquired of Billy.

'Near enough,' answered Billy. The shopkeeper went to the trees
and proceeded to test the pears by squeezing and gouging with his thumb.
He decided they were not quite ready and said he would come back in
a couple of days. This he did, and he and his assistant picked the trees
clean—apart from a dozen or so which were left hanging on the tree.

'What about the few that's left?' asked Billy.

'Oh, they,' the shopkeeper replied. 'They ain't no good, 'cos they've
been squashed and got thumb-dents in um.'

Billy caught hold of the peak of his cap and shoved it to the back of
his head, thus allowing his thumb to scratch the poll of his napper. He
replaced the cap with a jerk.

'Well, I dunno,' he mused, 'but I fancy that *you* were the bloke that
done that to um!'

'Ahhh . . .' replied the shopkeeper, 'It don't matter *who* done it to
um, Billy,—tis just that *they* ain't no good *now*!'

I ask you, what could Billy say to that? After all, he had been around
horses long enough to know about shutting the stable door, hadn't he?
So the deal was closed.

'Be the pears ripe?' the shopkeeper enquired when he returned the
following year.

'Ah, they be. Look alright, don't they?' replied Billy, and he wasn't
having any of it this time. He stood firm between the shopkeeper and
the trees.

'Ah, they *look* alright, Billy, but I can't *tell* properly from all over
here, can I?'

'No, don't s'pose you can,' said Billy with a thoughtful frown.
'Alright then. Let I hold thy hand and I'll let thee feel um!' Ahhh . . .
Billy-go-deeper, they called him. Folk called him that because they
couldn't get to the bottom of him.

Life with Vather

I think the widespread drunkenness of the thirties was a form of chronic depression. Most folk were poor and unemployment was rife.

Vather was a Boot and Shoe operative, and was employed at Clark's Shoe Factory in Street. Each weekday morning he would report to the factory in the hopes that he might be asked in to do some work. If he was unlucky, it was the next milk cart home, or Shanks's Pony, and he would then feverishly study the racing page, re-smoking his Woodbine dog-ends, wondering where his next pint of cider would be coming from. Should he prove lucky and land a couple of hours work at the factory, it would benefit the pubs and the bookies far more than his family. His money was *his* money, and we managed on what he felt he could afford.

He wasn't a big man. About five-foot-seven and slim built. He was greedy, self-centred. He was also a loud-mouthed, argumentative, quarrelsome, bad-tempered yob! He had once been a local footballer of some repute, and tended to bathe in the admiration of his past, and this made him stupid enough to spend his last few coppers on another drink so that he could hear the magic words, 'Good old Swiggy'. We, at home, would bear the brunt of his disillusion, disappointments, and the misery of his hangovers.

With no work, there was always the dole—and not a lot of that either! There were times when there was neither. The short spells of work made men greedy and suspicious. Another man once took Vather's work (I know the other man to be a greedy, grasping type, because I have worked with him.) This man said it was a mistake and Vather thumped him, anyroad. They were both suspended with no pay.

I did not hate my father. I was brought up with a sense of values. 'You can only take out what you put in.' The less you give, the less you get! Had Vather been like Pete Dennis, the cat with three legs, he would still have been 'our'n' and would be placed in a position of status as judged by each individual.

I once wrote in a compsition at school, 'I love blackberry and apple pie.' 'Miss' winged in on this like a half-bald crow. I loved my mother,

37

father, my brothers, but I didn't *love* apple and blackberry pie, she told
me. I *liked* it, she said. I looked at her in amazement. What was all this
talk about love?—And why was she talking to me about it in front of all
the class? We never mentioned the word in our house. I kept my eyes
down on the desk top. (Talking to me about all that rubbish!)

'I'm talking to you,' she said. 'Who do you love most in your family?'

'The dog, Miss,' I replied.

'Haven't I told you?' she bellowed. 'You can't *love* a dog, but you can
be *fond* of it . . . Let's put it another way,' she said. 'If your father and
a dog were drowning in the river and you only had time to save one of
them,—who would it be?' I gave this some careful consideration. Our
Tacks kept the rats down and she was worth about three rabbits a
week. That was three family dinners. She was also good company and a
good protector.

'Please, Miss,' I said, 'Who's dog is it?' Had 'Miss' used a little more
patience and designated that the dog in the river would be our dog,
instead of clouting me one round the chops, it would have been a cut
and dried answer of 'Goodbye Vather,' I'm afraid. 'A daft question to
ask in the first place!' I thought.

One couldn't talk to Vather. He would listen to argument, reason,
logic, and proof with a face etched in boredom and disbelief, and then
repeat his original statement word for word. When he talked it didn't
make much sense either. He was a liar, and don't get me wrong—there's
nothing wrong with a good liar—but he believed his own lies! He could
talk for ages and tell you nothing. Take the time he was telling me about
. . . Well, I think it was something about himself and Uncoo Awby . . .

'We were walkin' up town and we were talkin', s'no . . . And I said,
"Be you tryin' to listen to what I'm sayin"?—Walkin' behind I like that!"'

'To Uncoo Awby?' I asked.

'No. Our young'un was 'long with I, weren't ur?'

'Who, then?'

'Smiggit Smart! Now shut thy mouth and listen, will 'ee?'

'But I didn't know that, did I?—You didn't say.'

'How could I? I were goin' to tell thee, weren't I?—But you kept on
chammin'—in your half-pennuth. Anyroad, I said, "Let he get on up-
front," and he said, "I can't abide that scufflin' behind I like that."'

'What—Smiggit Smart?'

'No. He'd gone on, hadn't ur?'

'Then, Uncoo Awby were scufflin' behind, then?'

'Ohhh . . . Our young'un were still with I!—That's who I were talkin' to, so he couldn't be behind—not if he were still with I, could ur?'

'But you said somebody were scufflin' behind, Vather.'

'I know I did. That's why I were tellin' thee. Do thee listen, will 'ee? Our young'un said, "Let um go up front."'

'Who?'

'*Awby* said to I!'

'*Who* were scufflin'?'

'They-two young'uns!'

'What two young'uns?'

'Now looksee here. How can I tell thee summat if you keep-on stoppin' I? You'm like the rest of um. Won't listen when somebody's tryin' to tell thee summat!'

'Well, what happened, then?'

'I've got to go and call for our young'un now, or I shall be late gettin' there. I'll tell thee summat one day—when you've got time to listen, that is!'

'When *I've* got time? Our Vather,—*you'm* the one who's goin' on! What about all that scufflin', then?'

'Scufflin'? . . . That happened a long time ago . . . That were a bit of a laugh, that were . . . I'll tell thee about it one day. And as for I "goin' on"—t'will be a long time before I do "go on", let I tell thee!'

Hard to believe?

Let me tell you this one, then, of a time when there were a lot of witnesses present. As I have previously informed you, there were eighteen pubs in town, and Vather had been chucked out of most of them at some time or another for bad language, bad behaviour, or drunkenness. Sticker Lacey, landlord of the Rose and Crown, had banned Vather for life and he received this sentence as if he'd been placed on the Honours List.

He had to go up in front of the Legion Committee for causing trouble. They must have taken about twenty years to arrive at this decision, so it just goes to prove that someone did listen to him sometimes.

The charges as to why he had been brought before them were explained to Vather, and they then asked him if he had anything to say. Some folk are awed with official committees, but not Our Vather! He had a hard enough job of trying to understand his own kind, and any form of officialdom was automatically rejected the moment it passed his eyelids, thus leaving his mind a comforting, continuous blank sheet on which he would write his own fantasies.

'Ah,' said Vather. 'There is summat I'd like to say to thee . . . I'd like
to say three things . . . First thing . . . If you weren't in the Last War, you
don't know what you'm talkin' about! And . . .' (crooking his finger
beside his nose) . . . 'they what do run with the foxes do run with the
hounds.'

They waited for a moment . . . Nothing happened. The committee
man prompted,

'And . . . ?'

'What?' said Vather.

'You said "Three things". What were t'other?'

'T'other what?'

'Look—you said you wanted to say three things. You said we didn't
know what we were talkin' about if we weren't in the last war. That's
one.'

'Not like that, I didn't!' said Vather.

'TWO! You said, they that run with the foxes do run with the hounds.
Now, what's t'other?'

Vather looked at him in sheer amazement.

'Can you tell the difference between a fox and a hound?' he asked.

'Ah. I can!' replied the committee member.

'Well, maybe you can,' replied Vather, 'but you can't count very
good, can 'ee?'

I don't know whether the committee let Vather off, or just chucked
in the towel. I don't think that Our Vather ever knew, either. I don't
think he ever thought about thinking about it!

There you are, you see. You can get to like Good Old Swiggy.

Our Mother was pretty good with a sewing machine. She had had a lot
of practice. Mrs Snooks, down the road, wanted a lady's dress unpicked
and made into a smaller girl's dress for one of her daughters. Mother
sent down to the local shop in our road. The shop was in the front room
of one of the stone houses. Mrs England's house, it was. You know—Old
Regg'o's wife? She sold groceries, sweets, fags, baccy, and odds and
ends. There were those cardboard-boards of Stother's stuff in little round
bottles; Camphorated Oil, Olive oil, and Syrup of Figs in their little
elastic loops to hold them in place. Halfpenny and penny pencils were
on the same kind of cards. Biscuits were kept in cubed biscuit tins—and
you bought the biscuits without having to pay for the extra packaging.

The reel of cotton cost tuppence. It was a biggish reel of cotton.

Mother set to—unpicked the dress, and made the other dress to a

newspaper pattern. She charged Mrs Snooks a shilling . . . Reasonable
. . . Mrs Snooks was satisfied, and Our Mother was tenpence up after a
good day's work.

Vather scrounged a tanner from her to buy five Woodbines and a
pint of cider. ('Well, he had been working so hard on the garden, and he
looked so fed up.') On his way up town, Vather went into the local shop
where he got ten Woodbines on tick and left Mother to pay the fourpence.

Good Old Swiggy, he was such a good laugh. He would spend out on
booze. He'd throw it away on the horses. He lost, and he won, and then
there was more booze.

Wastrel? No, not Vather. I never knew him to waste a halfpenny on
his wife and kids!

But Christmas time? . . . Surely? Ah, yes. That was different. That
was when Vather got more drunk—more often.

Learning

I came into the house crying, looking for a bit of well-earned sympathy.

'What's wrong with you now?' Mother asked.

'Buggle Martin has been and hit I,' I told her.

'Serve thee right,' she said. 'He's bigger than thee. Pick on somebody thy own size!'

Our Uncoo Awffy grinned at me, and when Mother had gone out of the room, he beckoned me and said, 'If you go back and give him a good hiding, I'll give thee threpunce to go to Pictures s'afternoon.'

'But he's bigger than I be,' I said, 'And you always say you'll give I summat, but you don't never do it.'

'Give him a hidin',' he said, 'and I'll give thee threpunce.'

I went off down the road. Buggle was playing with my elder brother and his friends. They didn't want little kids hanging around with them.

'Who's the biggest fool down here?—Buggle Martin is!' I shouted.

Buggle ambled to the middle of the road, and we shaped-up to one another.

('Dodge out of the way and then hit t'other,' is what Uncoo Awffy always told me.)

Buggle's arms flailed like a windmill gone mad, and his fists seemed to be everywhere I happened to dodge-to. He caught me a couple of beauties and I felt my first experience of being 'knocked puggoo'd'.

('If you get hurt, get in close and hang on to have a bit of a rest.')

I closed in and grabbed Buggle about the waist. He hit me again and I found myself hanging onto his knees. Buggle seemed to want me a little lower down than this because he continued to rain blows upon me.

I returned to Uncoo Awffy.

'Can I have me threpunce please, Uncoo,' I said. 'He've gone home cryin'.'

'Get on with thee!' he replied. 'You couldn't make he cry. He's too big for thee.'

'But I have, honest!—We had a fight and I won!'

'Not by the state of thy face, you didn't . . . No. You ain't havin' I like that!'

I ask you, what can you do?—He was always like that.

There was a knock at the door and Mother went to answer it.

'Hilda,' we heard Mrs Martin shout, 'your Raymind's been and bit a gert big piece out of my bwoy's leg!'

'Then you better tell him to keep his legs away from my bwoy's face in future,' Mother hollered back. 'Anyroad, he's bigger than my bwoy. (Goin' home and tellin' his mother like a gert babby!) . . . And then, thee comin' up here with thy shoutin' . . .'

There was a little more arguing which gradually faded to the front gate. It didn't come to anything because we had the champion house-wife in our house, and she came back in and gave me a dose of the boiler stick for causing so much trouble.

'What do 'ee keep on doin' it for?' she asked me.

'Don't know, Mother,' I said, rubbing my fresh bruises.

'What do 'ee mean, "Don't know"?'

"'Cos I don't, Mother,' I said.

Off she went, leaving me with a grinning Uncoo Awffy.

'There you be,' he said, and gave me threpunce.

'But, Uncoo,' I said, 'I've just had *two* hidings for this!'

'Ah, I do know that,' he replied, 'but you only get threpunce for winning. Hidings don't count, do um?'

I suppose that was fair enough.

Our Mother wouldn't let me go to the pictures. It didn't matter very much, because Shirley Temple was on and I couldn't abide her at any price.

I had asked Gramf for a halfpenny for some sweets. He couldn't oblige. He was sorry, but he didn't have a brass farthing and would be broke until pay day. And I was asked not to 'look down' like that when we were talking to one another. 'Look down'?—I had to 'look up' at Our Gramf, 'up there'. Yes, he knew that, but there was 'looking' and 'looking at'. What could he mean?

It seems, when he was a boy, there was another little boy who was better than average, and he decided to get on in the world. He worked hard, became successful, employed lots of workers, and earnt lots of money. He was a good boss and was always fair to his workers. One day, he stood up-top his pile of money to get a better view of the world he was living in. (Feeling very proud, he was.) He 'looked down' on the folk who had helped to lift him 'up there', and he noticed they were 'looking down' on *him* from 'down there'.

'How can this be?' he wondered, so he asked his Gramf. His Gramf told him that that was up to himself, and that if he chose to 'look straight' at the folk 'down there', they, in return, would 'look up' at him from 'sideways on'.

And was I going to earn lots of money for my Gramf when I grew up? No, I didn't want to be rich like that other boy.

'Careful, me dear,' said Gramf. 'You've just started "looking down" again.'

—And I was looking 'both ways up' at Gramf at the time!

Why did the men with horses appear to be a little more brainier than the others? Gramf was a bit of a philosopher at times. Perhaps they had time to wrestle with their problems whilst travelling from one place to another.

I remember when some changes had been made at the Railway Station, and some orders had been issued from the head offices with no consideration or regard to the local problems they created. I heard him tell Mother about it.

"Tis as I've always said,' observed Gramf. 'The bigger the organisation— the less there is of it!'

I created other problems for him, too.

'How old is "OLD", Gramf?' I once asked.

'Cooh! That's a hard un, that is . . . Now let's have a think, a minute . . . "OLD" is when you start sayin' the same things . . . over and over again, more often!'

I didn't understand.

'No, you don't, not at your age, me dear,' he said, 'but you will one day, because that's summat that comes to us all.'

Haymaking with No Lemonade

One of the milkmen did the haymaking in the field down by Middle Lamp. There was a big mound in the field and we tended to regard it as a special place for us to play. The milkman recruited some extra help from the young lads in our road, and off they went with their heads held high in an air of new found pride and importance, disapproving strongly of the usual following of useless, noisy young'uns.

The milkman was also a small-time farmer of a small-time smallholding, yet lived up to the name of the 'greats' in farmers. He was dead stingey!

We young'uns were given small menial tasks to keep us out of the way, but we did as we were bidden. The milkman's wife arrived carrying her baskets, and the workers were called in for refreshment, and they made a lot of unnecessary noise refreshing themselves, because there was no bread and cheese, no sandwiches—not even an apple for the young'uns. We were too young, the milkman told us. We knew we were too young for the cider, so could we have some lemonade? No, he didn't have any lemonade . . . Then, could we go and fetch some bottles of lemonade from the shop? No we couldn't, because he had no money, and anyroad, lemonade was no good for growing youngsters.

A little later on, I heard the milkman talking rather excitedly to Our Mother.

'Have they young'uns brought any cider home—here, Missiz?'

'No, Jarge. They haven't brought no cider home—here.'

'Do 'ee think they've drunk it, Missiz?'

'No, Jarge. They don't like cider.'

And Mother was right—we had hidden it!

From the nearby copse we saw the new supply of cider arrive and, realizing that the search was over, we collected the gallon jar and three flagons and went in search of Old Regg'o. We found him working in the barn in Farmer Clark's farmyard. He was both pleased and perturbed by the gift, and chuckled when we told him why we had taken it.

'Haven't they missed it yet?' he asked.

'Ah, they have. They've got some more now, and they'm keeping their eye on it a bit closer.'

'And did anybody see thee come down here with it?'

'No. We come the long way round.'

'Right, then. Here's threpunce for some Tizer. Now, I want thee to leave here without anybody seeing thee, and go back the long way round.' His wish was our command, and we finished up honours even—plus a bottle of Tizer.

Old Regg'o returned the empties to Jarge a few days later—more out of the sheer devilment of the situation than out of honesty, I'm sure.

We weren't there at the time, but you can imagine how tales are told within a small community, and we had only to listen to the grown-ups to discover how we had fared. They approved because the milkman was considered fair game.

'Jarge,' Old Regg'o said. 'I found these over by the copse.'

'They be empty,' cried Jarge. 'They were full when I lost um though!'

'And don't I know that, Jarge?' agreed Old Regg'o, 'but we can't leave things like that hangin' around for little young'uns to find, can we, Jarge?'

I *was* there when Jarge passed by in his milk float, and Old Regg'o shouted to him from a nearby field, though.

'Hey, Jarge! Have 'ee got any more cider that you want I to look after for 'ee?'

Jarge could swear with the best of them when folk laughed at the pain in his pocket. It made Old Regg'o laugh like a drain. He would slap his knees—bend deep—then throw back his head and haw-haw again. He yanked his yarks up comfortably to resume his work.

'Off you go to play, now—there's a good dear,' he said to me and, as I departed, I heard him say aloud to himself, 'Oh, dear I. Good old Jarge!'

I have broached the subject of 'telling up a tale'. How those tales seemed to travel in a small community.

We thought Old Arrter was going to stay single all his life. He never seemed to be interested in the women folk, and he *was* getting on. Then, all of a sudden, he started courting Old Annie, and she was no chicken, neither. This gave our road something to talk about—but in a pleasant, comical sort of a way, because most of the folk were very happy for them.

If you saw them out together, you just *had* to look!

Arrter stood about five-foot-three, and he must have 'fetched' about seven stone with a good dinner inside of him.

Annie was a different kiddle-of-fish altogether—sixteen stone, if she was a pound! And I expect she was 'upsides' of six-foot-four in her sand-daps. (She had to wear these because they didn't make ladies' shoes wide enough to go on her gert big spavvins.) I heard-tell from a shoemaker that this was because they did not breed cows big enough to produce the hides, but I don't know the truth of this, mind.

Anyroad, they went for their evening walk together as usual, and it was noticed, on their return, that Arrter's pocket had been torn right down to the bottom of his jacket. The folk wondered, but no one asked. This was because they realized that, if they did find out, the real reason might not be as interesting as the one *they* had thought of.

I went over to the stone houses to see Our Gran.

'Have 'ee heard about Arrter gettin' his pocket tore?' she asked me.

'Ah. I've heard summat about it, Gran,' I said.

'Well,' she said, 'I hear Arrter were full of the joys of spring, and he give Annie a tap and shouted "Touch". As he started to run off, Annie give un a quick touch back—and hit un straight-through-hedge!'

Now that's perty good for an old un, isn't it? When I met Awbry I said to him,

'Have 'ee heard about Arrter's pocket?'

'Ah,' he said, 'Arrter told Annie that if she trusted him she'd let him carry her purse for her, so she give'd her purse to un and he put it in his pocket. As you know, Arrter do like his drop-o'-splash, so when they come by the pub Arrter said, "Oh, do thee look at thiick sunset, Annie, me dear." Annie looked and, while she were doin' it, Arrter nipped across-road and in-pub as fast as he could go, and he catched Annie's arm in the swing door and tore his pocket!'

Do you see what is happening? We now have Our Gran, Awbry, and myself with two different yarns to tell to everyone else—or so you think.

We saw Chols coming towards us.

'Hey, Chols,' we said, 'have 'ee heard about Arrter?'

'Tore'd his pocket, haven't ur?', said Chols. 'See, t'were like this here. Arrter got Annie to go up to the wood, and that made Annie think a bit, s'no, 'cos 'tis springtime, ain't it? He told her he just wanted to show her the rabbits, but she went along with un just the same. When they got there, *he really wanted* to look at the rabbits! Well, t'were all quiet and lovely up there, s'no, so Annie grabbed-hold-tight of Arrter and give un a gert big hug. Arrter couldn't get away 'cos he couldn't get his feet down on the ground. 'Oh, Arrter,' she said, 'I can feel thy heart beatin',' and all of a sudden there were this-here rippin' noise! Arrter said, "Annie, me dear, that weren't me heart what were beatin'. You've just woke me ferret up and he've gone straight through me jacket pocket!"'

Well, there you are, you see. You have all these good stories to tell, but everyone keeps on telling you one of theirs. It can be terribly frustrating.

'Good marnen, you three.' (It was the vicar with his bits of Somerset dialect.)

'Oh . . . Mornin', Vicar.' (You can't tell him, can you?)

'You look as though you have a secret 'tween the three of 'ee, there.'

'Well, it ain't a secret really, Vicar,' I said. (It's no good. I had to tell someone.) —'only Arrter's been and tore his pocket, and . . . !!'

'Oh, yes,' he said, 'I heard summat about that. You see, what really happened, was this . . . They were both comin' to church yesterday, to see me about the bans, and . . .'

Getting Around

The main method of travel to and from the town was by Shanks's Pony. Most of us used to run—not a mad rush, but just a steady sort of jog-trot. When it was cold, it kept you warm. When it was hot, you got there quicker.

And why not run? There was so much to do, with so many distractions —and unpunctuality was a crime. We ran to be there on time,—but only just. We ran to get the first and best choice of what was offered. We ran to keep out of trouble and, eventually, we just ran . . .

There were other ways to travel—with risks. Run to catch the tail-board of a fast moving horse and waggon. Climb aboard and ride if the driver would allow. Hang on tightly to the tailboard and slide—or pretend you wear those seven league boots and take huge . . . long . . . strides as you are pulled along. Dive beneath the rear of the waggon and lie belly-down on the dusty axle—but first make sure the driver has no dog, for this was their domain, and farm dogs guard zealously. The slow ride, a little faster than walking, could always be found with the timber waggons. The square long pole which stuck out from the two rear wheels was a natural invitation, and the layer of mud, snow, or crisp white frost on its surface didn't seem to disturb our thoughts of comfort or a free ride.

Loaded haywains were dodgey. It was always a slow plod. True, the driver could not see you, but the forward-lean of the load made sitting on the shafts a lesson of discomfort, so they would often walk on the curb-side of the horse. To discover who was riding on the back of the load, the driver had only to stand still on the pavement to allow the hay-wain to pass him, and the hanger-on, with his face buried in hay, would know nothing until he felt the sting of the whip or the withy stick. Hence the expression, 'Give un the withy!'—Belt him one!

Floats and traps were definitely out if you knew the driver was waging war on hitch-hikers. The tailboard of a float can easily be reached from the front, and the driver of a trap tends to sit close to the back.

There were other reasons why we were discouraged from these free lifts. There were the natural dangers of being knocked down, run over,

falling off, falling under—but we had heard all these things before.
Another reason was when the farmers started to come into town with
their waggons loaded with sacks of cider apples. They usually started in
late September, and then the flood would fade to dribs and drabs in the
later months. The cider works was down 'Back Lane', close by to the
Saw Mills and the Railway Station. Too close to our area, it was. We
approached these waggons quietly, almost as quietly as the farmer
hoped to pass us without incident. We would force holes in the slack-
woven sacks to select the pale green apples which tasted less sour or
bitter than the others. Pennard apples were good cider apples, but they
tasted terrible no matter what their colour.

If the farmer used a haywain, you could be pretty sure there would
be loose apples in the bed. I don't know why all the farmers didn't
employ this method, because it certainly stopped their sacks from getting damaged. Perhaps they disliked the thought of unloading at the
cider works. Those wooden shovels were nothing like the metal ones
they were used to.

The great black covered waggons of the railway with the S & DJ. R paint
on both sides were a haven from the rain and biting winds. We were always
allowed to travel on these, and the drivers were always so friendly.

Never cadge a lift from a putt. They travel slow. They are easy to
catch, but putts and their loads seem to love having a laugh at unsuspecting kids.

The nightwatchman in the timber yard was an old misery, and would
not allow us to play in there in case we got crushed by the logs when
they sometimes slipped. His duty started when the day shift ended. Later,
he would nip up town for his supper in the Mitre, and when he returned
he was usually the worse for wear, dribbling words from a toothless
mouth along the stub of an old clay pipe—punctuated with the departure
of the dewdrops at the bowl-end. We called him 'Popeye'. He wasn't a
bad old bloke, but we could be as cruel as any normal children. Popeye
would return to the four-wheeled wooden caravan in the timber yard.
We gave him time to settle down to his night-watching knowing that the
cider would eventually win. We went to the railway stables, harnessed
one of the horses, hitched it to Popeye's caravan, and then towed it to
the coal yard beside the Railway Station. We then returned the horse to
its stable, unharnessed it, gave it another double handful of oats from
the bin, and departed.

We weren't there for the scene next morning, because those days
started very early, but there was a lot of talk about town.

I remember another horse-drawn vehicle from which no child ever stole a lift. It was a small pony and trap, and it was owned by the fattest lady in the world! She was rather short, and weighed about twenty to twenty-two stone. When she climbed into the back of the trap the shafts would rise sharply, the tension would build up on the belly band, and the poor little pony would take a step or two backwards on its toes. The lady would then sit at the back . . . and the front . . . and on both sides— all at once! I can't ever remember seeing the door of the trap being shut while she was in it.

Spare no pity for the little pony. He was young, healthy, and well looked after, and could easily handle that twenty-odd stone on wheels. He was probably happy in the thought that his heaviest load would never be more than the weight of that lady and the weight of the last meal she had eaten—there was no more room! Should you feel concerned, then share the awe of the local townsfolk when they would see the trap and its traveller upon the brow of Tin Bridge which hovered over our very busy railway line. There was some talk in the town regarding the fixing of a red flag to the top of her whip to ensure that the usually un-suspecting train drivers below would get ample warning.

We kids used to cross the Tin Bridge as well—by using the three-inch ledge on the outside . . . with fingers clutching the top ledge and the odd rivet or two—twenty to twenty-five feet above the railway track below. Should a train approach, we would hurry—to get to the middle in order to be engulfed in steam and smoke. It was like looking down on the clouds. Silly really, because we would never know the truth of it. It was all pictures and imagination with us . . . No, not us . . . Not really, we wouldn't.

Up to T'other School

When you were seven years old you had to go to the other school. St John's, it was called, and what do you think?—There was a church on the other side of the playground with the same name. It made me wonder if they built those churches so close to the schools in order to be called by the same name.

It wasn't a bad sort of school, and it was built much on the same lines as the other one down below. I wasn't too happy there at first because there was still a 'Miss' in charge. There would be another 'Miss' in the next class, as well, but seeing there were only boys allowed in this school, I didn't feel I could complain too much.

The first 'Miss' was old, with her grey hair done-back in a bun. She had Horned-rimmed glasses and a hairy wart beside her mouth. And like the last 'Miss' down-t'other-way, she had it in for me from the start. This puzzled me because reports from one school to the next had never entered my mind. I couldn't understand it, because all of the others had usually given me about two weeks grace at the beginning. This 'Miss' was always trying to ridicule me in front of the class.

She would let us take it in turns to read aloud. We would all sit at our desks, each with the same story in front of him, following the one who was reading aloud. There was one book in particular that I remember. It was a good one. All about Jack, Ralph and Peterkin on a coral island. They went down to a cave under the sea and they had to haul Peterkin down there because he couldn't swim. (Don't know why, because he had been on the island long enough to learn.) He started to struggle once on the way down, and that could have been dangerous.

Cooh! That cave! You ought to have seen it. The light came into the cave up through the water from outside, and the white sand helped a lot. They sort of came up into a quiet lagoon and landed on a little beach. I'll bet if they had looked around a bit more they would have found some smaller caves in there . . . If they had done so, they might have found some treasure in one of them which had been left there by pirates. There might have been a gert big octopus in another cave—just waiting for them, watching . . . with his one big eye . . .

Whop!--Someone had belted me one round the ear-hole!

'Miss' was stood there. 'Did you hear what I said?' she asked.

'Yes, Miss,' I replied. (I hadn't, mind.)

'Well then, go on and start reading, then.'

Ticker and Tubb were laughing at me. We always laughed at the one who got a hiding in order to try and make him laught so that he's get another clobbering.

'Ah,' I thought, 'You two can laugh, but I can read alright. I can read good. 'Tis just as easy as sums and writing, it is. Don't know why we have to keep on doing it, I don't. Now just you listen to this . . . This is the B.B.C. and "watch-out" Arthur La Dell, or whatever your name is . . .' I started to read and the whole class started to laugh. 'Hullo, then,' I thought, 'summat's gone wrong here.'

'Trust you to still be down in that cave,' 'Miss' thundered. 'Everyone else left there ages ago! What have I told you about that day-dreaming? Will you never pay attention? Ray-dream Burrows—that's what we shall have to call you.' (Oof! I'll best the rest of the class will love that one. I can't see them forgetting it very quickly, neither, judging by the way they are enjoying it at the moment.)

('Still in that cave,' she said . . . *Who* took me down there in the first place? . . . AND . . . *Who* went and left me down there? Blimmin' women teachers . . . I shall be glad when I get up in 'Sir's' class.)

It was in this class that I wrote my first piece of poetry.

> Blast it. Sod it.
> Blimmin' and damn.
> Somebody stole my rotten old pram.
> Don't care a bugger.
> I'll soon get another.
> Blast it. Sod it.
> Blimmin' and damn.

I won't claim the author's rights for that one, but write it, I did, on a piece of paper which had been supplied to me by 'Miss' to stop my grubby hands from making a mess of my book whilst I was writing. She had also given me a cardboard 'spacer' the width of a forefinger, to assist in the spacing of the words, but I had chewed that to bits in one of my meditative spells.

I passed it to Ticker, who passed it to Tubb, who passed it on . . . It

reached one of the well-dressed boys who's mother kept a shop in the
High Street. He didn't like me, and I seemed to have a natural aversion
to all of his kind. He held the piece of paper up in front of his face and
tittered loudly, and pretended to look surprised when 'Miss' ordered
him to deliver the epistle to her desk. It was readable, so that eliminated
fifty per cent of the class, and it was not long before I was off on my
first visit to the headmaster. His classroom was the same as all the other
classrooms I had seen, apart from the different objects hanging and
pinned to the walls. He was a very business-like man, I'll say that for
him. He glowered at the poem. He glowered at me.

'Did you write this?' he asked.

'Yes, Sir,' I said. ('Here we go,' I thought. 'Now he'll say, "Why?",
and I'll say, "Don't know, Sir"'.)

'Sir' must have thought, 'If I ask him why, he'll say he doesn't know,'
so he went to his cupboard, got out his thin cane, and gave me two of
the best on each hand. I got my second dose of the cane on the afternoon of the same day. Three on each hand for fighting. I'd caught the
tattle-tell during the dinner hour and split his lip, and he hadn't told
on me this time. 'Miss' had noticed that his nose wouldn't stop bleeding
in class, and the rest was pure deduction.

The next class up had a 'Miss' as well. Oh dear, it seemed to me I was in
her class a very long long time. I thought I had finished with her sort in
Class II down-t'other-way. She was old, and middle-aged along with it.
She was plumpish . . . chubby and saggy in the cheeks, and wore her
horn-rimmed 'sperticles' in a 'skew-whiff' sort of way. Her hair was red
. . . going to grey . . . going to white—or grey and white going red. It
seemed to be bundled up in an untidy ball and looked as though it was
likely to fall apart at any moment. 'Looks as though thiick mop of her's
could do with a touch of the bandy,' one of the farm lads commented
to me. (A bandy is a hooked stick to hold the grass clear whilst using a
reap hook.)

The sums, the reading, and the writing was alright—but she and her
blimmin' mat-making! Yes . . . We had to make bastick-mats with rafia.
Blokes knitting mats!—I ask you, now! She told us that the blind folk
made them. I tried to do mine with my eyes shut. She came around to
see how things were going on, and she rattled my knuckles with a
couple of one-foot Somerset County Council Education Committee
rulers.

'It looks as though you have been doing that with your eyes shut,' she told me.

Then there was that gert big wall map of her'n. She kept it rolled up on the wall. She would then pull a string and down it would come with a rattle and a clatter. Frightened me to death the first time I heard it! A map of 'WE', it was, and she would stand beside it with a long pointed stick with a 'proper handle on'. She would point . . . she would tap the map . . . she would scowl at us over her wobbly glasses . . . and she would shout until she was red in the face. I don't think she liked this lesson much, either. She never struck us with that stick. No, as I told you, she would rattle your knuckles with the rulers, she would thump you in the back with her fists, and she would slap you round the chops, but that stick was for poking that 'Map o' WE'.

Tap . . . 'Jersey', we would shout. Tap . . . 'Guernsey', tap-tap . . . 'Alderney and Sark' . . . Tap . . .

Oh, God, I used to hate this.

Tap, round and round . . . 'Orkney Islands', tap . . . 'Isle of White'. Tap . . . 'Isle o' Man'.

Hated it!—HATED IT, I did!

Tap, and round . . . 'Scotland'. Tap, and round . . . 'Wales'. Tap . . . 'Ireland'.

Don't know why I had to do it. I was never going to go abroad, any-road!

We were hoarse. We were tired. Torture-time over?—Not on your life! We had to take it in turns to point out where we had been for our hol-idays. Most of the class groaned, but I wasn't worried about it because I had only been to Burnham. I even felt a little pleased when my turn arrived. Out I went, collected the other poking-stick without a proper-handle-on . . . Ah, there it was . . . Thought it had moved for a moment . . .

'No—not that one, you don't!' said 'Miss'. 'You've had that one for the last three weeks . . . Where's Peterboro?'

'Peterboro, Miss?—I haven't been there!'

'It doesn't matter if you haven't,' she said.

('That's good of her,' I thought, 'and to think that I . . . !')

'Show me anyway,' she said.

Well, that was it. She'd completely broken my concentration with her underhanded ways, hadn't she? Ohhh . . . That blimmin' Map!—All those places on it and I bet every one of them had a different name. I pointed and tried to look as though I knew what I was doing.

'Oh, well done!' said 'Miss'.

('Not really, Miss,' I thought, 'Just a good guess, I think.')

'I am amazed,' she said.

('And so you should be, too.')

'Amazed to think they have moved Peterboro to South Wales without
informing anyone about it!' she went on. 'Don't you ever listen to anything I tell you? Go and sit down, and remain after school . . . Leslie,'
she said, 'come and show us where Peterboro is, please.'

(Please?—And I bet he'll be able to do it, too. I bet his mummy and
daddy have took him there as well! Teacher's Pet, and I hadn't never
know'd him to have a patch on his trousers, yet . . . Always dressed
'smiggit', he is. You know the type—clean hanky every day, and all
ironed up, and he doesn't have to unfold it to blow his nose, neither!)

(Right, Leslie . . . You show us, but I'm not going to watch you, not
with you doing it, I'm not . . . And don't laugh, me son . . . some can,
and some can't!) I kept my eyes glued to his face. He didn't laugh. He
didn't smile. He didn't smirk—but he looked pleased with himself—just
as though he knew where it was without looking at the map.

As we passed one another between the desks, he fell over! I sat down
quickly in case 'Miss' thought it was me—and she did. She rattled my
knuckles on both hands 'right proper'. Oh, it hurt. I kept my eyes and
head down as I blew and rubbed my fingers, and stole a quick glance at
Tubb and Ticker. They were sniggering fit to 'bust'. I grinned at Tubb
and he burst out laughing. 'Miss' grabbed hold of him with one hand
and a couple of rulers with the other. Something must have upset her,
you know, because she didn't half let poor old Tubb have it. I watched
his face with his eyes 'squinched' up, and then his mouth seemed to go
into a little 'oo' and travel up the side of his face to just below his right
ear-hole. I could restrain myself no longer. I burst out laughing and
Ticker caught the fever. 'Miss' tackled Ticker, and Tubb came back on
our side.

Rattle, rattle, rattle, thump, thump, thump . . .

It was no good. The more cross she got, the more helpless with
laughter we became. I really wanted to stop because she was hurting
me, but it was hopeless. In the end we finished up with Tubb behind one
blackboard, Ticker behind the other, and with me stood up on my dest
(desk). This was the worst place to be because the others flipped ink-
pellets at my legs and 'Miss' was able to see my face all the time.

Headmaster was busy, so I had to see him after school, next day.

Flying High

Kites were always popular. Even the penny waxed-paper kites with the printed smiling face was given a fair chance, but the paper was usually too fragile and the tails were never long enough. Some would fly well. Most of them would not fly at all.

There was always the same feeling of apprehension for the new kite. (Had I got a good un this time?) There was only the one way to find out. Some would twist and turn with no intention of ever leaving the Mother Earth. Some would fly for a short while and then the corner would break from the cane frame and come crashing to the ground. Others would fly well, then suddenly dive earthwards for no reason at all to land with the same old sickening thud. A good one could last a whole day.

Uncoo Awffy made us a beautiful box-kite for no reason at all. A kite as grand as this was never meant to fly from the mound. No, this one was worthy of the top of Weary All, at least. It would fly for miles from there. More string was needed. There was some in the sideboard drawer, and we couldn't use the white string because that cost tuppence a ball, so we made-do with the penny-halfpenny ball of brown string which seemed to be made of twisted cardboard.

The kite flew. There didn't seem to be much wind about, but we could feel the sudden jolts of wind up there from nowhere. One end of the string was pegged to the ground, and we would hold spare loops of string in our hands. These would be passed to another, one hand at a time, when we 'changed go's' after our turn had expired.

Suddenly, without warning, the brown-paper string gently floated down to lie kiteless on the hillside. No hillside, road and field had been covered so quickly since the day Ken Bridges was chased by a swarm of angry bees. Uncoo Awffy would help us . . . After all, it was his kite, really . . . He would know how to get it down. He came out of the house shouting, 'Alright, Alright!' and looked to where we pointed.

There above us was the Graf Zeppelin!—We hadn't seen it's approach and, even though I had not seen one before, I knew it was German by the markings on its tail. Read any comic or boys' magazine.—All the spies and villains were Germans. Read Our Cousin Ted's war magazines—

57

all about our aeroplanes and the German ones. Listen to the war tales of
Vather—all about the German shells, the German snipers, the German
barbed-wire, and the German black bread in the German prison camps.
Those Germans were a bad lot!

Uncoo Awffy looked up with some concern. The kite was flying
high—too high for Uncoo Awffy, even.

'Hope thiick-there kite don't bump into thiick airship,' he said. 'If
he do, we'll have another war on our hands, I 'spect.'

The thought of it filled me with horror. I'd really done it this time! I
studied his face . . . He was a master at pulling my leg, and he didn't
laugh. I watched with mouth agape, heart in throat, and hands 'clinched'
as the kite drifted closely to the Zeppelin . . .

Our Uncoo Awffy knew it all, he did.

'Looks as though he *might* miss . . . but you've got to take a count of
the wind,' he said.

An aeroplane flew close to the Zeppelin . . . It was going to machine-
gun it, I think . . . It didn't, and we watched the Zeppelin slowly dis-
appear over the crest of Weary All.

In the meantime, the kite had gone.

I found a soldier's rifle in our back garden. It was brand new and clean,
nothing like as rusty as the old musket that Tubb played with.

How had it got there? Where had it come from?

I looked up and saw hundreds of German balloons and kites, and
German soldiers were parachuting down from them all over the place.
One of them landed in our backyard by the coal shed. I would have to
shoot him, of course—but was the gun loaded?—Was the safety catch on
or off? I didn't know how to tell. I'd have to let him get close, and then
I'd clonk him one with the rifle butt.

The parachute rolled away in a ball of hot, dry wind and the soldier
stood up. Grey uniform, jackboots, and a small pillbox hat. He had a
moustache. They all had a moustache, didn't they? He saw me with the
rifle and put his hands up in the air . . . Then he laughed as he saw me
fumbling to get hold of the barrel to slosh him in cowboy style. He
grabbed hold of the butt to wrench it away from me . . . It exploded . . .
without making a noise

Phew! I climbed over Our Young'un, who was sleeping next to me . . . I
pushed him to the middle of the bed and settled in his place to sleep again.

. . . and I flew my kite . . . One of these paper ones, it was . . . A pinky-red colour. I flew it from the top of the mound, and it flew well, far better than any of the others had done . . . Higher and higher, it went . . . It started to jerk at my hand very strongly, and I had almost taken a step forward when I realized that the ground had fallen away, leaving me standing on a tall pillar of earth shaped like a factory chimbly-stack!

As I glanced down the world tilted and suddenly lurched! I felt the stack buck and dip away from my feet!

The terror of attempting to get myself off of those fumbling feet . . . I tried to get down onto one knee and the kite kept on tugging me off balance so viciously. 'Don't look anywhere,' I thought . . . I closed my eyes and felt everything spin rapidly outside of my trembling eyelids. Still, at least I couldn't see anything . . . God, it's dark in here . . . Think . . . think . . . and then–'I wonder if there is still enough ground behind my feet!' Had I moved? Had I staggered? . . . and the kite kept on tugging . . .

I opened my eyes and the wind blew so hard and warm. The kite went mad like an eagle trapped by the tail . . . Round and round it pulled on its length of string . . . Could I hear it screaming?–It was hard to tell with the roar of the hot, dry wind. Down onto both knees . . . hands and knees . . . I almost rolled over! I lay face down, fingernails and toes dug into the short, dry, snapping grass . . . the dusty grass . . . I couldn't breathe . . . The soil crumbled over the edge from the sole of my right boot, and I struggled to find another toe hold. With a shriek, the kite wrenched my hand free from its grip on the soil. I couldn't pull it down again . . . and my right hand was slipping . . . The pillar began to crack across the surface . . . Sand and grass flowed into it like liquid . . . I dug deeper with toes and fingers to close the crack together.

I could see German airships and balloons–like flopping, wallowing, silver ghosts coming across the moor with the setting sun behind them.

The Germins were coming!

I must get home and warn Mother. We must hide!–Yes, HIDE . . . I must lie still for the moment . . . Let them go by, and then I'd go home . . . But they saw my kite. They could hear it screaming like a dozen seagulls! They thought I was waving . . . and I couldn't let go . . .

I could hear the moaning, groaning, drone of their engines as they came towards me like concertining maggots lolloping and nosing through the cloudless sky like greyhounds with no legs . . . I couldn't cry out, there was too much sand in the air . . . It was too hot . . . I couldn't breathe . . . I would have to let the kite go . . .

I slowly tried to open my hand . . . it did so . . . so slowly . . . The
kite wrenched my fingers straight . . . the string tangled tightfully and
painfully about my fingers . . . and pulled . . . and pulled . . .

I couldn't let go!

I stood on the crest of Weary All . . . I jumped to catch a piece of
brown string which hung from the clouds and, as I grasped it, it jerked
taught, and swung me outwards and downwards towards the moor. The
string was thin. It cut my hands, but I managed to scramble higher to
fly over the top of the oak trees at the bottom of the hill. I was going
faster and faster . . . and lower. Lower? Of course—as I got to the
bottom of the swing I would go lower, wouldn't I? . . . I climbed some
more . . . I could hardly see because the rushing warm wind made my
eyes water . . . The speed forced the breath out of my body . . . I
climbed frantically once more to avoid a brimble bush . . . My hands
hurt, and I couldn't breathe, but it would be alright when I got to the
bottom of the swing—But where was the bottom?—Was there a bottom?—
Would I be too high up the string when I swung back over Weary All?
. . . The pain in my hands . . . Could I hang on long enough to get back?
. . . and I couldn't breathe . . .

I stood on the crest of Weary All . . . I jump to catch a piece of string
which hung from the clouds . . . Hey, wait a minute!—I've done this
before! . . . and I am already swinging towards the moor . . .

I stood on the crest of Weary All . . . I see a piece of brown string
hanging from the clouds . . . I have seen this before . . . I know I have
seen this before . . . and I am swinging towards the moor once more. I
shall not touch it the next time!

A couple of weeks later the kite was found out on the moor. I was
glad to see it back because it was such a good one. 'Did I want to play
with them?' they wanted to know . . . I told them no, and that I'd got
summat better to do. Nothing in particular, really, but anything was
better than a kite at that moment.

Visiting Days

The local police would call at our house at irregular intervals, and these visits depended on the state of our luck. Some of the times it was just to make enquiries, and other times to tell us that they had made enquiries and would like to hear our side of it.

There were also warnings of trespass and for general mischief—like taking rides on the sewer sprinkling system. It was a huge four armed pipe in the shape of a cross which revolved slowly to sprinkle water onto a bed of clinker and cinders. They could be persuaded to go a lot faster. I gave Our Young'un a good, hard push on there once, and he whizzed round to the other side—straight into the arms of the factory foreman.

It must have been close to the beginning of November because I had found an old armchair that had been thrown into the field behind our houses to be burnt on the bonfire. I had managed to extract four of those spiral upholstery springs and was attempting to tie them to my feet, after which I would be off—jumping from field to field like Spring-heeled Jack in the *Hotspur* . . . or was it the *Wizard*? Might even have been *Chips*. No, that was Captain Kerrigan . . . *Comic Cuts*, then? . . . Oh, I can't remember.

Our Mother called me from the upstairs back window in a rather ominous voice. It's funny how one learns to detect the sound of a black look, isn't it?

I went home to find a Copper's bike leaning against our front hedge. The owner was sat on the sofa in our front room, and still wearing his cycle clips. He had taken his helmet off and had placed it on the floor beside him.

He was there because I had been playing in the factory yard and had found six empty glass, acid-carboys and they were placed in metal basket-like containers padded with straw. I accidentally knocked one of them and was impressed with its melodious note. I tapped the next one. A different note! This had to be tackled properly. I found a twelve-inch length of metal pipe with one end enclosed in a piece of hose pipe. The ideal thing. I tapped the carboy . . . Yes, just the job.

Have you ever tried to play 'Rock of Ages' on six empty carboys? It

doesn't seem to work very well the first time, does it? I couldn't
seem to get the right pitch, so I tapped a little harder . . . No . . . A
little harder . . .

Have you ever tried to play 'South of the Border' on five empty carboys, then?—It's impossible, no matter how many times you try. And
it's no good trying to play 'God save the King' on the four that remained, so I went off and found something else to play with.

I found that this was the usual way of getting into mischief. I had no
intention of doing any damage, and seldom realized I had done it until
it was pointed out to me.

Mother settled out of court.

Another Bobby came to see me on another occasion. I had been
stealing cauliflower. I hadn't been caught or seen, but some of the others
had been caught on the way home, and one of them must have told. One
of the other culprits had a mother who owned a shop. She said her son
didn't like cauliflower, and all those who didn't have a mother who
owned a shop got 'tabbed'. I had learnt another lesson. Work on your
own!

Our Mother settled out of court.

Our Young'un and I crossed the field from our house to the Main Road.

The Council workmen had gone to dinner, and the nearest pub was a
long way away. This upset our plans a little, because we had had our
dinner and had come to watch them working. The power of the two
folded red flags intrigued us. We had seen them at work. There was also
a spare green one.

Very little motorized transport passed along the Main Road in those
days. We stood in the middle of the road with our flags. I faced in the
direction of town, and Our Young'un towards Street.

This was hard work. After about ten minutes of hard flag wagging I
had three cars, a lorry and a horse and cart lined up beside the road. I
turned to check up on Our Young'un's feeble attempt—Six cars and two
horses and carts! How did he manage that? After all, I was older than
him. Oh, well. Perhaps I'll be able to catch up in the next ten minutes . . .

Our Mother saw us from the kitchen window. Our Vather bellowed
from the back garden, and we dropped our flags and shot off up over
the side of Weary All like a couple of startled bucks! On arriving at the
top we looked back to see the two small lines of stationary traffic, with,
no doubt, some very perplexed drivers, wondering what they could do
with a pair of discarded red flags.

'Could they follow us up there?' Our Young'un wondered.

'No, dafty. There's a wire fence at the bottom, isn't there?'

'Couldn't they go to the gate and get in?'

I hadn't thought of that, so we rushed up to the copse out of the way.

From the top of Weary All there is a marvellous view. Close to the back of the hill the Roman Way runs parallel to the hill, and houses were built on each side of the road.

We would throw stones just to hear them clatter down the roof tops or just to see if we could hit one roof in particular. Had one of those stones fell short it could quite easily have killed some unsuspecting, irate resident as he charged out into his back garden. The thought of broken tiles never entered my mind.

We brought roofing slates from the building tip at the foot of Weary All on the other side. A roofing slate is fairly heavy, so we would snap them in half and then throw them into the wind and watch them glide. I can't ever recall watching one to see where it landed.

When the Copper called at our house, it wasn't for the sole purpose of seeing me. I mean, what are brothers for?

There was a loud knock-knock from the brass knocker on our door.

'I'll go!' we shouted, scrambling to get to the door—not because we wanted to answer it but because we liked to see *who* was knocking. We rushed squabbling into the passage, and then braked as if suddenly threatened with a shotgun. Through the six frosted panes of glass in the upper part of the door we saw the shape of a policeman's helmet!

Closely followed by two younger brothers, I rushed out of the back-door, across the gardens, over the fence, and out into the field, and as I ran I tried to recall what I had done wrong this time . . . There was nothing! I asked my two brothers, and the lying little sods told me that they hadn't done nothin', neither. They wouldn't tell me if they had.

We decided we were not hungry at teatime, and stayed out until bed-time in order to give Mother enough time to forget all about it. It was a very worrying two or three hours for all of us. We could put it off no longer, so we went indoors, went quietly into the backroom and commenced to take our jackets and boots off. The rest would be taken off in the bedroom—apart from the shirt, and we slept in them.

Where had we been until this time? . . . Nowhere. Just playin' . . . Were we hungry? We hadn't had no tea . . . No, we weren't hungry . . . What had we been eating then? . . . Nothing . . . A piece of bread and dripping each, and we were sent off to bed. It had worked!—Or, had it? —We still didn't know why the Copper had called.

We found out the next morning.

It is here that I feel I ought to inform you that my elder brother spent most of his time up at Our Aunt Kate's, and was often referred to as Aunt Kate's Bwoy. This seemed to have a strange effect on him because he was never in trouble, never in a fight, and seldom in an argument, even! The kids down our road had given up all hopes for him. I had sort of taken over as ring leader of the kids in our family, and I was continually being harangued with remarks such as'

'*He* never does bad things like that'.

'Why didn't I behave like *him*?'

'Why don't I try to be like *him*?'

'Oh, *he's* a very well behaved bwoy, *he* is'.

Well (and I don't expect you believe this), *HE* got caught riding a bike with no light—and they summonsed him!

There he was—only ever did one thing wrong in his life—the only fully fledged criminal with references in the family!

Did they call this justice?—After all, I had worked hard for my reputation!

A dark horse in still water, that's what he was!

The Hardship of Drawing

I always liked to draw, and it was no good doing nothing if you felt like doing something, was it? I pondered on my problem—the same old financial problem. I could get a notebook and pencil from the local shop, but that would cost me a penny and I didn't have one. It was hard to find a halfpenny at that time of the week. No one wanted me to run any errands . . . I wouldn't be getting a penny off Our Gran until I took her shilling club money to the shop next Sunday morning. What can you do without money?

As Our Mother said, 'There ain't a lot of it about.'

There were some big iron wheels in the burnt-out Old Mill. Iron on the outside, with a lot of white sort of cemented stone on the inside. Heavy great things, they were, and some of the stone was cracked, and if you could chip a piece of that off it made very good chalk. We used it for hopscotch. That would do, wouldn't it?

Have you ever tried to draw a ship three houses long? If so, have you ever tried drawing it on a road in the middle of summer? It's very hard work, let me tell you. That tar may look good and hard at first, but it sticks to your knees and hands when you crawl on it. It can be removed with lamp-oil. It can be removed with butter as well, so I'm told. We never had butter in our house. If you sit in the tar, that's it. You get stiff-seated trousers then. It feels like armour with no shine to it, but that wouldn't stop Our Mother from trying to give them a bit of a burnish whilst the occupant was still in them.

'What do 'ee want to do that for, anyroad?' she asked. 'Bide there, makin' a mess!'

'I were only playin', Mother.'

'Ah, so *you* say! . . . Upsettin' folk, here.'

'I didn't upset nobody, Mother.'

'Oh, didn't 'ee?—What about Missiz Juggs, then?'

'Oh, *SHE*!'

'And Missiz Jack!'

Well, there it is . . . You can never do anything around here without both of them getting on to you. They must have told Mother 'round-back' so that I wouldn't be able to hear, thus preventing me from making an early getaway before Mother's intervention. There I was drawing that ship. I'll bet it was the biggest ship that had ever been drawn down our way, too ...

'And just what do 'ee think you'm doin' there, then?'

'I be drawin' a ship, Missiz Jack.'

'A ship?—It do look a tidy mess to I, s'no.'

'I dunno, Missiz Jack. It do look alright to I.'

'Don't you be cheeky with I, young feller-me-lad! I shall tell thy mother on thee. I said that that do look a mess, and that's what 'tis! Outside folks' houses, here ...'

'But you've only got the back-end of him in-front your place, Missiz Jack.'

'And that's more'n enough! Ain't that a mess, Missiz Juggs?'

'Ah, that's a mess alright ... A right blimmin' mess ... Why don't 'ee go further down the road and make thy mess down there?'

'They "down there" told I to come up here and make me mess outside me own house, Missiz Juggs.'

'But this here ain't *thy* house, is it?

'I started off by our house, Missiz Juggs, but he were too long.'

'Then why didn't 'ee go t'other way, then?'

(If they hadn't looked so cross, I would have laughed, s'no!)

'I can't do that, Missiz Juggs. Can't 'ee see? This here, is the back-end of the ship. I can't go and put the back-end on the front-end just 'cos it goes past thy place, can I?'

'Right! That's it. I'm goin' to see thy mother—thee see if I don't! Never seen such a mess, I haven't. Never in me life!'

'But, Missiz Juggs, you said, only t'other day, that there were nothin' worse that thiick steam lorry down-bottom of the road kickin' up a smeech!'

'Ah! But that chawk stuff on the road do make horses shy! Don't it, Missiz Jack?—Don't it make horses shy?'

'Ah, that's what it do do ... 'Opscotch do make hosses shy ... Thy mother's goin' to hear about this, thee see if she don't ...'

'But, Missiz Jack. T'other day you said that Our Gramf's horse did make more mess than anythin' else around here!'

'And that were only until you come along here with thy mess! I've told thee, and that enough!'

'Aw, Missiz Jack ...'

Hopscotch!—That ship didn't look anything like a hopscotch. That ship was a good un, and it was hard work with all that tar sticking to you.

'It'll frighten the horses,' she said.

It didn't frighten Our Gramf's horse . . . Come to think—judging by what he'd left there, he didn't think anything of it at all! Yes . . . A blimmin' gert heap, right where the ship's floor went up a step at the front-end. I had only just got halfway through the dockyard refit when Mother came out and demanded the return of her coal shovel. 'It wasn't for playing with,' she'd told me.

('And who's '*She*'?—The cat's mother?')

I had to move the rest with two fag packets until they got too soggy . . . (Too much linseed, I think, Gramf . . . Probably needs a bit more chaff) . . . I then resorted to the only two available tools I had left . . . It'll wash off . . . one day . . . Those fag packets . . . 'B.D.V.', they were . . . You know, the ones with the cricketer's pictures printed on the back instead of fag cards? I'm glad I wasn't Jack Hobbs . . . Can't remember the other bloke—and I bet he's glad!

Hullo? There's Our Mother at the front gate. She looks wild about something to me . . . As you can imagine, it wasn't one of my days.

A belt with the boiler stick wasn't always the punishment. Have you ever had to push your baby brother in a pram, up and down the road for hours and hours, just to keep him quiet? Well I have, and proper soft I felt about it, too! These were the times when I wished I had an older sister.

I had intended to go down to Acky Dock with the dog . . . All t'others had gone . . . But, no, I *had* to push the Babb for a while . . . How long is a while? I went in and asked if I had done it long enough, and was told that I would have to do some more 'for comin' in and askin''. If I hadn't asked they'd have forgotten all about me, anyroad, and I'd still be there pushing the pram.

With mixed feelings I watched Mrs Juggs and Mrs Jacks come to their front gates for their hourly ten minutes of 'chim-cham'.

('Oh, dear I,' I thought. 'Here we go, "Oh, isn't ur lovely!"')

'Takin' your little brother for a walk, then? Helpin' your mother, be 'ee?'

'Ah, I be, Missiz Jack'.

'Come here and let I have a look at un . . . Ohhh, don't ur look lovely . . . He do look lovely, don't ur, Missiz Juggs?'

'Ah, he do look lovely alright, Missiz Jack. Betterer, and a bit more cleaner than his older brother, anyroad! He don't look nothin' like t'others, do ur?'

'I 'spect that 'cos he's only a babb, Missiz Juggs, don't you?' I said.

. 'It ain't what I do *"spect"*, young feller-me-lad. 'Tis what *you'll* make him into! Such a lovely babb, too . . .'

('And so he might be, but that won't stop thee from tellin' him to keep outside his own house as soon as he can walk!')

'Poor little dear . . . Don't stand a chance, he don't. He don't stand a chance, do ur, Missiz Jack?'

'Hey, but I haven't done nothin' wrong!' I said.

'You don't need to!—You've already done enough to last thee a month or two!'

'Ohhh yeeesss . . . Just thee wait 'til Missiz Bert gets her hands on thee . . . You'll be sorry . . . He'll be sorry, won't ur, Missiz Juggs?'

(Cooh, what have I done now?—Get blamed for everything, I do!)

I was glad to depart from the two old dears. I wondered if their husbands kept on saying like Our Vather, 'I'll be better off out of it!'

Hullo—as if things aren't bad enough. I'll bet these two girls have a go at playing 'grow'd ups' . . . Always betendin', they are . . . Why don't they get on with their skipping, or do some of that 'round-knitting-through-the-cotton-reel' stuff? Bide there, grinning at me . . . Look out, here they come . . .

'Ohhhh . . . Takin' the baby for a walk, then?'

'Ah, I be, and I've got a long way to go . . . !'

'Oh, look at un blush. He's shy, I think.'

'No I ain't. Not of *thee*, anyroad!'

'Don't thee take no notice of her, Ray. Let I have a look at the babb, will 'ee?'

'Ah, well . . . I'm in a bit of a hurry, s'no, and . . . !'

'Ohhhh, isn't ur lovely?—Do thee look, now. Look just like his brother, he do. Look at un, Jane.'

(Blimmin' girls. They won't never listen to nobody!)

'I don't want to look at thiick babb if he's anything like *he* there!'

'Oh, get on with thy hopscotch, thee! I don't 'spect he could bide thee close up, anyroad!—Blimmin' girls!'

'Ohhhh . . . Hark at he, now. Don't half get upset quick, don't ur? Have Missiz Bert seen thee yet?—She do want to.'

'What for?'

'I don't know, do I? Why don't you go and ast she?'

'Hey. Get thy head out of thiick pram! Do 'ee want to give the young'un a fit, or summat?'

There goes Herby ... I haven't got to play with him because he gets
me into trouble all the time. And there's Mrs Wills and Mrs Wick having
their usual 'ha'puth' of news three doors from one another. Here we
go, just listen to them stop talking as I walk past. Hullo ... Mrs Chubb
has jambed her letter-box open with a ball of newspaper again. That
should cramp their style a bit, anyroad.

'Missiz Wills' ...

All gone quiet, it has ... I'll bet this slow pace of mine is killing
them ... Shall I stop to fix the tyre on the pram wheel? ... No, they're
looking fit to bust, already, and I shall only mess it up if I laugh ...
Won't be long now, me dears ...

'Missiz Wick' ...

There you are—they're off and at it again. Don't know why they
bother to stop talking because they could talk over the top of a thunderstorm.

Mrs Juggs and Mrs Jack down t'other end of the road were laughing
their heads off when they heard Mrs Wills talking about her husband's
bad back, again.

There's Gord ... He hasn't got to play with me because I get him into
trouble all the time ...

'Hoy! Come here, you!'

Mrs Bert wanted to see me, I think ... She was nasty and loud-
mouthed when she was in a 'nice' mood.

'I be takin' the babb for a walk, Missiz Bert ... !'

'I can see that, can't I?—Come here when I tell thee!'

'Yes, Missiz Bert ... '

(Cooh, she looked upset, alright.)

'What have you been up to, then?'

'Nothin', Missiz Bert ... I've been takin' the Babb for a walk, and... !'

'I know all about that! Now ... Who else were up-there be the hayrick playin' Doctors and Nurses with Our Ivy?'

'It weren't I, Missiz Bert!'

'Hah! I dunno about that—but I shall find out—thee wait and see!'

'Well, it ain't I! I don't play with girls, 'specially thy Ivy!'

'Don't thee cheek I, you snotty-nosed little arab. You want to learn
some manners, you do. I'll see thy mother about thee, thee see if I don't!'

'Well ... '

'And what do 'ee mean,—" 'specially Our Ivy'"? Come on, what do
'ee mean by it? She's too good to play with thee, let I tell thee! Don't
know what the blimmin' kids is comin' to around here, I don't!—And

don't walk away when I'm still talkin' to thee!—Come back here!'

I'll bet Mrs Wills and Mrs Wick had their money's worth there ...

Doctors and Nurses? I'll bet that was Herby. He's the one for playing those kind of games ... It was *him*—that time they were playing schools—and I got the blame for that as well! Herby ... Our Gramf said that he wouldn't trust him with our goldfish when he gets a bit older.

Oh, the blimmin' tyre has come off again. I tied it on with a bit of decent string, too! Even the dog has left me ... Can't say I blame him, there's more fun down Acky Dock with the others ...

Getting – for Going

'Here, pop up town for I, will 'ee. I'll give thee a halfpenny for goin'.'

And what could one do with a halfpenny, one would ask? Do?—I could spend a farthing with no feeling of shame.

A longish mile up to town, and the longer, loaded mile back for a halfpenny, the good old halfpenny. Yes, I would go. It was a fair, popular offer for the UP TOWN trip. Two farthings—one halfpenny. Two halfpennies—one penny. Four farthings—one penny. It was all money. Some folk said the farthing was no good any more, and this puzzled me. I once asked the little man—who sold boys' suits for 4/11¾d, and socks for 5¾d—Why—if the farthing was no good? He told me to mind my own business, young man. Funny old world, isn't it?

We young'uns would run these lucrative errands for most of the folk down our road, and our clients would soon sort themselves out into their appropriate categories. There were a few in the generous bracket— one whole penny if the load was a heavy one. Then came the old reliables who would promptly pay their halfpenny on completion of the delivery. There were the habitual 'I haven't got no money at the moment. I'll let thee have it later on' ones, and the 'later on' would take so long that the errand-runners would band together and approach the culprit whilst she was in conversation with her neighbour, and politely request she settle up.

'What?—The four of thee?—I can't afford tuppence. Here's a penny between thee!'

How do you share ten toffees between four children? We had no pocket knife to cut two in half, and our rotten milk teeth were not up to the task neither. Two boys would be selected to suck away the first half (and no chewin', mind!), and at some indiscernible point of sucking the second halves would be transferred to the other waiting pair.

Money deals were the straightforward deals.

There were those who could not afford to give us money, and the fee would then be a piece of cake, a stored apple (a delicacy out of season), or a piece of bread and jam. There were the financial downfalls when the family breadwinner would find himself on the dole once

more. They wouldn't tell *us*, but Our Mother would direct me to go up
town for Mrs Wills and 'don't take nothin' for it', because they couldn't
afford it at the moment. And they *couldn't afford it*. No, not even a
good old halfpenny, which was worth two farthings, which was worth
nothing.

Aunt Ider loved to make generous offers whilst other grown-ups were
listening.

'Go up town for I, and I'll give thee tuppence for goin',' she'd squawk.

The neighbours, of course, were never within earshot when the
errand was completed in Aunt Ider's kitchen.

'Have a piece of cake for now,' she would say, 'and I'll let thee have
the tuppence later on.' But she was so forgetful, poor dear.

I would have done the trip for the piece of cake, but it was the act in
front of the neighbours that stuck in my throat. I took the piece of mushy
cake and hurriedly carried it to my greedy mouth—but not quick enough!
Before the first bite had passed my lips, she would say,

'You don't get that up home, do 'ee?'

She would *always* say something like that!

A copy of Landseer's 'Lord of the Glen' hung on the wall, and the 'Lord'
made no effort to disentangle his antlers as the cake slid down his glazed
features in slow-sliding, squodgey lumps.

She would tell Vather, she told me, and I didn't care.

When Aunt Ider gave, she did so to the imaginary fanfare of golden
trumpets. 'How good she is,' the neighbours thought smilingly . . . And
here was I with Aunt Ider's latest offer for another town trip.

'No,' I said, 'You didn't pay I last time.'

'Oh, you nasty little sod!' the neighbours would look.

'Didn't I pay thee?' Aunt Ider exclaimed with well practised child-
like innocence. 'I must have forgot.'

'And not for the time before that, as well!' I shouted.

'And she, always bein' so good to they young'uns, too!' the neighbours scowled.

Poor, affronted Aunt Ider . . . They felt so sorry for her . . . Oh, she
did look hurt. She would see Vather. He would make me go! Yes, he
would—but that was the difference. *He would   have to make me go.*

Vather came out from Gran's house all ready to go up town on an
important mission. He was a punctual man and liked to be there before
they opened. My behaviour was an infringement on his religious activities
and, quite naturally, he was a little upset. A quick cuff on the back of
the head, accompanied with an apology for not having the time to take

his belt off to do me full justice, preceded the instructions to go up town
for Aunt Ider, and I was to get nothing for going.

'Same as I got last time!' I shouted to him and the neighbours, taking
care to dodge the second clout round the chops.

Trumpeter, sound off!

Aunt Ider posed like a spoilt brat, folding one arm across her flat
chest, and, touching her cheek with the forefinger of her other hand, she
would deliberate. She wanted a piece of lean beef for Sunday . . . About
three and sixpence worth . . .

There came the expected gasp of admiration from the onlookers. 'All
that, just for the two of um!'

('Why did they never save it for the second act?' I wondered.)

Aunt Ider would dramatically ponder, and then, with an angelic
smile . . . 'Better make it about four and sixpence worth . . . and some
lites for the cat.'

I repeated Aunt Ider's order to the butcher in front of a shopful of
customers, and, with no small amount of satisfaction, I added in a loud
voice, ' . . . and a pennuth of lites for Aunt Ider.'

The randy old butcher repeated it in an equally loud voice and grinned from ear to ear. He played his customers along like a professional
comedian. He loved to keep his customers happy, and happy they were.

'Pardon, Missiz?–Do I keep drippin'? No, I "went" just before I
started work, and I shall be "goin'" again when I do stop for me cup o'
tea. Nice of thee to ask, anyroad.'

The lites were wrapped in newspaper and would stick to them in
soggy blotches when they were unwrapped. The beef joint was cut and
tied, and then placed on a piece of greaseproof paper. He would shout
the price and weight to his mother in the 'money place', and she would
write the bill. It was a small white bill and the butcher's name and a
sheep was printed on it in dark blue. The bill was then affixed to the
meat by means of a wire pin which looked something like a half-opened
paper clip with a zig-zagged shaft. More greaseproof paper was placed
around the joint, and then beef and lites were wrapped in the one newspaper parcel. A work of art from start to finish.

I stood on the kerb by Market Place . . . thinking . . .

Vather was in-pub safely out-the-way . . . Aunt Ider had won hands-
down so far . . . Our Mother wouldn't take any notice of Our Aunt Ider
if she went up there moaning about me . . .

I took a long length of string from my pocket and tied one end about
the parcel. A lot of frustration from unpaid errands, broken promises

and bare-faced lies disappeared as I flopped the parcel into the dusty,
partly dung-strewn gutter, and from there, with a slow deliberate tread,
I dragged it home to Aunt Ider's front gate. Her front door was always
open and, if one bothered to peer closely through the gloom, it was
possible to see the dark-brown painted door of the coal house at the far
end of the passage.

In true bolas style, I whirled and whirled the joint about my head
and then hurled it the length of the passage where it collided with the
hollow door with a contented and very tired 'FLUMP!'

I couldn't run away. I had to stop to see Aunt Ider's face. She was
going to tell Vather . . . I knew she would. And I was going to get a good
hiding for it! . . . I knew that, too. With head held high I passed along
the row of condemning scowls that had appeared with the commencement of Aunt Ider's squawking.

I felt good. Aunt Ider would never ask me to run another errand.
. . . which was just as well.

We were playing marbles in the gutter, and the grit and glass-allies were
knocking spots and great chunks out of my dull-coloured clays.

'Come yer.'

I looked across the road in the direction of the voice. Old Harr
stood there. He wasn't a big man, 'tall-wise', but it could prove fatal to
call him small. He had had a bad bout of rickets as a child, and his feet
had stopped at ten-to-three of the clock ever since. There he stood in his
best navy blue suit, and it wasn't Sunday. Black, shiny boots, collar and
tie, a new trilby; there hadn't been a funeral, and he was looking at me.

'Come yer,' he said again.

To study Old Harr's face was a waste of time. Rain or shine, his dark
brow carried a frown as deep as a well, and his boney face expressed an
age-old scowl as wide as the moor. His brown-black, simmering eyes
glared at me.

'What for, Harr?' I asked.

You see, when Harr looked at you like this—and he always did—you
never knew *how* he was looking. I mean, I could size up a snarling dog,
and knew whether to move in on him or 'leave him be', but, with Harr,
one would automatically think to one's self, 'Hullo? What does he want
me to do?', or, 'Have I done it wrong already?'

'Shan't tell thee again. Come yer!'

I cautiously crossed the traffic-less road—not the 'right, left, and
right again' kind of thing because my mind was concentrating on a far

greater kind of danger. My whole attention was rivetted on the face of
Harr. He may have been slow on his feet, but he had fast hands to
match his quick temper. Curiosity killed the cat, and a hand shot out
to grab me by the shoulder. It wasn't a fair grab, his countenance hadn't
changed one bit! He glared at me as his other hand appeared from his
trouser pocket.

'Here's a penny of that tuppence I owe thee. I haven't got no more
small change at the moment.'

Of course! I'd taken his boots up town to be mended, and had collected them a couple of days later. I had forgotten all about it, and was
so delighted with my new found source of wealth, I decided to cry
quits.

'Thanks, Harr,' I said. 'Don't worry about t'other penny. We'm
"snicks" with this one.'

'I didn't say nothin' about no snicks, did I?—I said I'd pay thee later
on, didn't I?—Blimmin' young'uns and their snicks!—*I'll* say when we'm
snicks, alright?'

'Alright, Harr. Thanks very much.'

'No need to waste your money on he, Harr.' Vather, followed by
Uncoo Awby, had arrived on the scene.

No one listened. I stared unblinkingly into the unblinking, smoulder-
ing, dark eyes of Old Harr, who obviously had something else to say to
me because the grip on my shoulder had not slackened. My whole attention
was focussed for the slightest sign of relaxation in the vice-like grip. A
quick twist of the body and I would be out of range, but the opportunity
did not arrive. We had both been brought up on the same ground.

'And I don't want any more of this "Ten-to-three-the-feet" when
you'm out-in-field out-the-way.' 'Tis funny when your Uncoo Taff says
it, 'cos all-they-Welsh blokes have been fed on pit-prop-pie and don't
know no better, but 'tis rude comin' from a young'un. Alright?'

'Right'o, Harr. Sorry.'

'Sure?'

'Jonick!'—And the truth can't be more truer than that, can it?

'Now,' continued Harr, 'Off you go and spend your penny before
somebody around here scrounges it off of 'ee. *And*', he turned to address
Vather, 'What I do with my money is *my* business—nothin' to do with
thee—but if you'm on the mooch for a drink, come on, I'll buy thee
one.'

Vather's pride had long been swallowed with a gulp of cider, and he
followed Harr like the dog he was. Uncoo Awby stood motionless with

mouth agape—whether in astonishment at Vather's new-found source
of wealth, or at his failure to word or wave a goodbye, I shall never
know. Harr stopped and looked back at him.

'Well? Come on, Muck-Face, if you want a drink!'

I don't know why he called Uncoo Awby that, neither, because he
always had a sloosh in the mornings and a hot wash and shave every
night. Our Vather only shaved on Fridays.

Oh, I almost forgot. I haven't told you why Harr was attired in his
best suit and chucking money about in the middle of the week, have I?
Same again, I'm afraid, I don't know! I mean—if he wouldn't tell a
'grow'd-up', like Vather, he definitely wouldn't tell a cheeky, snotty-
nosed, young sod like me, would he?

No . . . Harr's business was always Harr's business, and, as I said, you
never knew with Harr!

Up and Down like a Burn'um Dunkey

As far as I was concerned, in those days, our Railway Station was only
there for three reasons. 1. It was somewhere for the train to stop. 2. Our
Gramf liked to work there with his horse. 3. That was where I would
catch the train to take me off to Burnham for my day's holiday, once a
year.

It was the Sunday School outing. I think we stopped going to church
because they never sent you anywhere unless you were a choirboy. Well—
not while you were alive to enjoy it, anyroad. There were personal con-
victions in my non-church-going, too. There was the occasion when we
turned up at the churchyard with our own spade and coal shovel in order
to bury Tobe's dog. The vicar wouldn't hear of it. 'You can't bury a
dog in a churchyard . . . Dogs don't have souls. They don't go to Heaven,'
he told us. 'No dogs allowed,' I thought. 'What kind of place can that
be?' Heaven became less and less interesting from that day forward.

It took Our Mother a lot of hard work for the day's holiday. You see,
the first of our tribe came along about half-way through the twenties,
and after that we seemed to add another one about every two years. After
a while, this habit began to be realized as a bit of a handful. Some of us
would need new suits—thin flannel suits of blue, grey, brown, or green,
with four shiny buttons on the jacket. It was the best one could get for
five shillings a shout.

So, come the big day with everybody ready to go, Mother would
muster us outside the front door. This was to ensure she would have someone to help her to drag the door to. It not only dragged, but jammed
against the door frame as well. We didn't lock the door because it would
take a strong man to push it open (poor old Vather when he came home
puggoo'd-drunk), and we had nothing to steal, anyroad.

The two eldest would carry the basket with the 'sambidges' in: cheese,
fish paste, and cucumber (all done up posh), with the bottles of lemonade and a borrowed flask.

'Do thee mind thiick flaxx in the bastick, you two! If you breaks he,

77

we shall be in the Workhouse, all of us!'

When the procession moved off the basket would lead, followed by the in-betweens, followed by Mother with the Babb in the pram. (She preferred the rear position because she didn't have eyes in the back of her head.)

On arriving at Middle Lamp without incident, we met Old Regg'o.

'Well, well, well!' he beamed. As lovely a brood as ever I've seen . . . How on earth do 'ee manage with um all, Missiz?' ('With a gert flat hand,' I thought to myself.) I said nothing, because I had no wish to ruffle any feathers before we got to Burnham.

The pram was left down-Station, and the train took a long time coming in. Gramf came along to see his 'dears' off and to give us a penny each to spend 'down there'.

The railway carriages had no corridors in them, and this proved inconvenient from the 'convenience' point of view but, at the same time, enlightened Mother's task of keeping a clutch on her clutch, holding us in one tidy heap for most of the journey. Those train rides were some of the longest rides in the world. Eighteen miles, it was, and it took up far too long of our day's holiday. We would eventually arrive smoke-stained and travel-stained . . . some were tear-stained . . . with Mother nerve-strained.

This is where the hard work started—'looking out' to us on a sandy, crowded beach. Battle preparations were drawn up to decide which part of the beach would be our'n for the day, and the boundaries would be quickly sketched in the minds of us all. We would then surround our last ditch with holes and sandcastles—the last ditch being, of course, Mother and the basket of 'sambidges'.

The 'Can I have' business would then commence. Mother would buy us two wooden spades, two tin buckets, and two bathing costumes. These costumes were like a vest with the bottom sewed up, and they were red'n'black, blue'n'black, green'n'black, and yeller'n'black. They were made of a very thin type of cotton material, and when they got wet 'they showed all our belongin's through' as Mother would point out with a shriek.

Come tea time, we would go to a big, posh hotel. Brown bread and white bread—both with butter on! . . . Jam . . . Plates piled high with buns, scones, and fancy cakes . . . Cups *with saucers*, and a plate *and a knife* for each person. The fact that we sat on benches at cloth-covered trestle tables did nothing to destroy the awe of being in a posh place. Our tribe had viewed the outside with reverence and had become self-

consciously quiet since we entered, and our unusual behaviour seemed
to put old Mother on edge more than ever. She said nothing, but would
govern and guide us with tight-lipped scowls and glares. Some ladies
would bring the tea around in big jugs, or big brown tea-pots with an
extra handle on the front. The lady that served on our table received a
thank-you from each of us and, on arriving beside Mother she said, 'Well,
you-lot have been brought up, haven't 'ee?' . . . and Mother kept on
looking at us.

Our seating arrangements were similar to the procession. Mother
would sit one end—the in-betweens in between—and the two eldest on
the other end.

Yazzer, a bloke from up town, was sat on the other side of me. He
was a couple of years older than I, and asserted this fact by putting his
elbow onto my bit of table. In true Sunday school style, I retaliated by
placing my elbow against his to push him back. This accomplished
nothing, apart from preventing Yazzer from advancing further into my
territory. I couldn't force him back because he was bigger and heavier.
I caught the warning raised eyebrows from my elder brother. 'Watch
out. Mother!' it said, so I immediately withdrew from the fray, placed
my hands in my lap, and sat up straight.

Just in time. Mother's gaze arrived just as Yazzer's elbow ploughed a
furrow in the table cloth in my direction, spilling cups of tea and rattling
the crockery, thus earning him a 'I'll see you later' look from his
mother . . . and I was being as good as gold.

Whilst the Sunday school bloke was saying a few prayers for all of us,
Yazzer nodded in the direction of the fancy cakes and whispered,
'Which one of they dost thee want?'

'I'll have he with the white icin' and the cherry stuck on top,' I
replied, thinking he was going to hand around the plate.

'Well, you won't get he, 'cos that's the one I'm goin' to have!' he
whispered.

Well . . . You can't be warned off like that in front of your younger
brothers, can you? I mean, I hadn't looked too good in the previous en-
counter, had I?—And now he had come to me with this little lot! Right—
if he wanted competition, he could have it!

As soon as the Sunday school bloke got to the last part of his 'Amen',
I didn't bother to give him one of mine, and I was in like a shot!—I
grabbed that cake! You should have seen the look I got from Our
Mother. She didn't turn her head, she just sort of steered her eyes sideways. I think she was too shocked to move. I tried to smarm her over

by breaking the cake in two and handing it to my two younger brothers beside me, but the look got worse and worse . . . Too late I realized I should have cut it with my knife, and I should have placed it on their plates, but their hands got in the way . . . Oh, why should I be blamed all the time? I mean, we don't have knives at home!

Still, my prestige had been restored. Yazzer thought I had broken the cake so that he couldn't take it away from me. The dunch fool. He was the last one I was worried about at that moment.

'I'll see thee after tea,' he said. Must be all that sea, sand, and salt air that make folk feel so good. I didn't feel too badly myself . . . I told him whereabouts we were sat on the beach.

Teatime finished . . . They gave us an orange each, and we returned to our old position on the sands . . . and along came Yazzer . . .

('If they'm bigger than you, try to catch um on the hop. Get the first one in.' Thank you, Uncoo Awffy . . .) I caught Yazzer half-way down a stone slope to the sands. We were over the side before either of us realized it. The fall hit all of the wind out of Yazzer, and, as he lay on his back gasping for breath, I topped up his mouth with sand and got stuck into him like a ball of barbed-wire.

There were screams and shouts from somewhere and I know they didn't come from Yazzer. His Mother and Our Mother came rushing in and neither one of them were on my side. I got hammered all the way back to where we had been sat before. Cooh, Our Mother were wild, s'no . . .

'Now sit and bide there quiet!' she said. 'Don't know what things be comin' to, I'm sure!—Fightin' down Burn'um!'

I was 'biding there quiet' when Our Young'un (two down from me), approached and informed me, 'Yazzer said, if his mother hadn't come, he would have gived thee what-for.'

'Then thee go back and tell *he*,' I replied, 'that empty churns do rattle loud. And if Our Mother hadn't been on his side to look after un, I would've show'd *he* the way home double-quick!'

He went off to deliver the message and on his return seemed well and truly convinced that I had come off best in the altercations. He offered me a soaking-wet, blue'n'black bathing costume.

'Here art,' he said. 'You can have my go, if you like.'

There you are, you see. This is what large families is all about. I didn't accept the offer because I had got my orders from Mother and that sea-water had been a little too cold and salty for my liking. Tide was going out again, anyroad . . . 'Burn'um on the Mud' we used to call that place.

The train ride home was even longer. The young'uns were tired and went to bed with less noise and fuss than usual.

'Shall I make a drink of cocoa, Mother?'

'Ah, you do that and I'll turn on the wireless.'

'Shall I light the gas or the oil lamp, Mother?'

'Leave um both out. We'll listen in the dark . . . Haven't got much left . . . Nice for a change, weren't it?–Goin' down Burn'um, I mean . . . (Better put some salt-brine on thiick eye of thine 'cos he'll be black come-morning.) The sea didn't look too bad, but t'were cold though, weren't it? Shouldn't like to be down there all the time though . . . All that sand . . . As soon as I heard all the noise and shoutin' down there, I *knew* one of mine were in it . . . Little buggers, I had to laugh afterwards . . . Well, 'tis over again now . . . Burn'um, the train rides, the lot . . . Nice to be home again . . .'

She sat in the armchair with one leg curled beneath her bottom.

Yes, Mother, it was a nice change. (Wonder why Vather never comes with us? There are lots of pubs down there, I've seen them.) Only another year to go and she will have scraped enough together for another day's holiday down there.

She must have spent every bit of a pound down Burn'um, s'no!

The Time Our Vather Saw the Light

Yes. That was a day, that was.

If you knew Our Vather, the first thing you would say would be 'I'll bet *he* never saw the Light,' but you would lose your money if you wished to make a real bet of it, though. You see, for those who knew him, it couldn't possibly be true. He would cuss, argue and shout when he was sober (which wasn't very often), and he would cuss, argue and shout a sight more when he was drunk. He would argue with anyone or everyone. It depended on who happened to be there at the time. If someone happened to agree with him—then there would be something wrong with that someone because Vather didn't like people saying the same things as he did. Should have someone prove to Vather that he was entitled to do so, and emphasise the point with a thump in the eye, Vather would never give him the credit that was due. No. It would be put down to the swing-door up-the-Pub, or because he had fallen over our front gate.

Had he fallen in the rhine once more he would have gotten himself webbed feet! No ... No, I'm sorry ... I'm wrong there. Vather didn't *fall* in. That rhine would flood its banks and creep out on Vather every time he happened to pass by on the way home—and that took some doing if there happened to be a drought on at the time.

Still ... This isn't telling you about the time Vather saw the Light. Just listen to this, now ...

It was about the time when they were putting the new sewer pipes in up through the town. They dug a great big trench about twelve feet deep and about six feet wide. All done by hand, pick and shovel it was ... Part of this trench was the width of the path away from the double doors of the Legion.

It was dark and misty when Our Vather and Uncoo Awby came outside—three parts slewed as usual. They always went to the pub together. They went to work together. They went everywhere together. I think this was because they were the only two blokes who could put up with them! They argued with one another, mind. Oh yes, argg'd all the time, they did.

82

Anyroad, they came out of the Legion and that was when Our Vather
saw the Light. It was one of those red ones that the work-blokes had
left behind. Some folk will tell you that Vather was a bit puggoo'd with
a couple of pints inside him, but, give him his due, he knew what that
light was when he saw it.

'Mind thiick light, Awby,' he said to Uncoo.

'What do 'ee want I to mind he for?' asked Uncoo Awby. 'They've
got proper blokes to do that job!' (Proper Union bloke our Uncoo was,
and Vather nearly smiled when he heard that.)

'Don't be so daft,' he said, 'I didn't mean "mind un" like that. I meant
"mind out" for un.'

'Then why don't you say what you mean if you'm goin' to say summat,'
said Uncoo, 'I do know what a red light is just the same as thee!' (Uncoo
Awby was almost a match for Vather.)

'I were only tellin' thee, weren't I?' said Vather. 'I were tellin' thee
'cos I saw un first, and not 'cos I thought you didn't know!'

'What do 'ee mean?' asked Uncoo Awby. '"If *I* didn't know what
t'were?"—You think you know so much, but if thiick red light had been
a white un, I'll bet you wouldn't have been so clever!'

Vather didn't say nothing, because he didn't never listen to nobody
who did keep on arguing with him. He dopped-all-dainty up to that
light like a gert big fairy with hobnail boots on.

'Ah,' he thought to himself, 'Thiick-light-there is a dangerous light if
ever I've seen one.' And Vather knew what danger was because he had
been keeping out of the way of it all his life. Which was what he meant
to do at that very moment, so he went and took a huge, high step
straight over the top of it! He landed flat on his back in the bottom of
the trench in about fifteen inches of water and white liquid clay.

'I s'pose you'm alright, aren't you?' Uncoo Awby shouted down to
him.

After a slight pause, Vather answered, 'Ah, I think so . . . Here. Help I
out of here, Young'un!'

Uncoo Awby said he couldn't because Vather was too far down to
reach.

'Then go back in-Pub, then!' shouted Vather. 'I be scrammed with
the cold down here, and I don't want to bide here all night!'

Uncoo Awby couldn't see the point in doing that. The bar had been
closed before they came out. He pointed this out to Vather.

'Well then, get on home and get somebody to help get I out then!'
bellowed Vather, 'I could have been there meself by now, if I weren't

down in here!'

Such a bad-tempered bloke he was. Uncoo Awby set off, and to see
him mugglen down that road you wouldn't have thought he had almost
a mile to go. You could never rush him, you see . . .

A little later, the Landlord and a couple of his 'special' friends came
out and I think they must have heard Vather's teeth 'chammin'' down
in the trench. The Landlord was a good man. He was always glad to see
Vather—in a situation like this. He was good natured and, when he had
had a good-natured laugh with the others, he asked,

'What be doin' down in there, Swiggy?'

The others, being as tender hearted as the Landlord, couldn't bear
to look, knowing that if they looked again their laughter might upset
Vather. One of them was a bloke called Nicker Simms, because he had
one of those laughs that made others laugh, and this could cause trouble
at times because Nicker would laugh if someone broke a leg.

'What be I doin' down here?' said Vather. 'What do 'ee think I'm
doin' down here?—I'm waitin' to get out, ain't I?'

. . . and then, with a change of heart which could always be found in
Vather whenever he found himself in a position where he couldn't help
himself, he pitifully asked,

'Here. Help I out, will 'ee? . . . I shall catch me death a cold down
here . . .'

'Why don't you climb up the ladder, then?' the Landlord asked.

Things went very quiet down in the trench for a while . . .

'What ladder do 'ee mean?' Vather asked.

'Thiick-there ladder what you'm holdin' on to!' they all shouted with
glee.

There was another slight pause before Vather could say anything.

'Cooh! I dunno, I'm sure . . . I didn't see he there, s'no! . . . No, darned
if I did. And Our Blimmin' Young'un didn't tell I he were there, neither!
Thee wait 'til I do see he next time!'

Nicker was all doubled up in a little, gasping ball, pleading with the
other to 'hurry up and get un out' because he couldn't stand a lot more,
and the others laughed and rolled about. They were just about getting
their breath back when Vather climbed out of the trench and started
them whooping and hollering again. And no wonder, because he certainly
looked a sight. Cold, wet and sober and covered from head to foot in
white clay. He looked like a snowman left over from the last 'falling'.
Landlord got his breath back . . . He cared . . . He was considerate . . .

'Awby ain't down in there, is ur?' he asked. 'I mean, you weren't stood on his shoulders, were 'ee?'

'No,' said Vather. 'He went home to get some help, but I 'spect he've forgot all about it by now.'

That started them off again, and Nicker pleaded with them to stop him in case he got a 'touch of the "sterricks".' Vather didn't join in. He didn't mind folk laughing at him if *he* thought it was funny. Well, there . . . He thought this little lot were acting up summat cruel! He thought he would put a stop to it . . .

'Oh! I think I've been and hurt me back!' he exclaimed.

That just about brought the house down.

Vather decided to get all serious about it. He could stand it no longer. He gave the red light a kick with his soggy boot and looked at them 'all stern'—just like a drunk judge would look at you.

'Now looksee here!' he said from behind his crooked finger.

They stopped laughing to listen with their teeth gritted tightly . . .

'That's a bloody daft place to leave a red light!' said Vather.

Alright Then?

Folk can be different. Folk can be kind—even those who get on to you all the time when you've done nothing wrong.

'Oh? Haven't gone to school today then?'

'No, I haven't, Missiz Juggs. I've got to go to hospital to have me tonsils out.'

'Oh, have 'ee? . . . Never mind, me son . . . I 'spect you'll feel better for it later on. He'll feel better for it later on, won't ur, Missiz Jack?'

'Oh, ah . . . He'll feel better alright.'

'But I don't feel bad now, Missiz Jack!' I said.

'Ah! I do know that, but I 'spect it'll make thee feel a bit better, anyroad. How old be 'ee now, me dear?'

'Sebben, goin' on eight, I be.'

'Ah well, that's like I told thee . . . It'll make thee feel better.'

I had never been in a hospital before and I didn't like the feel of the one I had been brought to, neither. I was in the same room as Chivv's mother. I went to school with Chivv.

Why was I in the same room as Chivv's mother? I told you, to have my tonsils out. But, why was I in that room? Because that was where my bed was. It was the only one they gave me, anyroad. Funny . . . Everyone seems to ask me that. Well, everyone apart from Our Mother. She seemed only too glad to see me in a bed! Well, I won't say she was *glad* . . . She was quieter. She didn't seem to shout or talk as loud as she did at home.

'Now mind you behave yourself,' she told me, and her old eyes did seem to roll behind those glasses of her'n. I was the first child of her's to go into a hospital, and you may think that she was a little worried about leaving me there. No, it wasn't that. That place frightened her to death! After Mother had gone I talked to Chivv's mother for a while, and she didn't know what it was all coming to, she didn't . . . She wouldn't have been in there if she hadn't felt so bad . . . No, she didn't know what it was all coming to, coming in there . . . No, that's true she didn't . . . Didn't know at all why . . .

They came in and took Chivv's mother away on a rolling-table.

This was the first time I had ever had a bed to myself. At home, I had
to sleep with two of my brothers. It was usually the two eldest on the
outsides, but with Our Young'un you couldn't do that because he would
sweat like a pig in the middle, so I would swap places with him to let
him cool off. The warmer I was, the better I slept. Well—not better—
heavier. We could cuddle in to one another to prevent either of the outside ones from falling out.

'Mother! Our Ray have pee'd all up the back of my shirt!'

'Oh? . . . Never mind . . . Take thy shirt off . . . I'll see about it in the
mornin'.'

'But 'tis gettin' cold now, and I shall feel cold without me shirt on!'

'Then put thy jersey on! . . . I'll see about it in the mornin'!'

Blimmin' tell-tit. He woke me, shouting like that! Anyone would
think I made a habit of doing it to hear him! I ask you . . . Can I help it
if I was dreaming I was 'going' down by the rhine?

There were other times when I had to sleep in the single bed in the
small room with Our Uncoo Awffy or Our Aunty Vere. When it was
Uncoo Awffy, you would never know he had been there because he
came in very late and left early. Aunt Vere used to leave her belongings
on top of the small 'chester drawers' when she went out courting for
the evening. She fondly remembers the time she returned late at night
to find me wearing her gold watch which had been given to her for her
twenty-first birthday. The innards of the watch was spread all over the
bed. There was also the time she came into the darkened room of burnt
celuloid to find that the imitation tortoise-shell handle of her vanity
mirror was now a genuine piece of scorched wood, and the suspicion of
a comb rested in the candlestick beside a box of burnt matches. I was
lucky. I was sound asleep on both occasions. Our Aunt Vere's right hand
could out-gun Mother's hand, the boiler stick, and Vather's belt put
together. One belt in the ear from Aunty Vere—and your feet ached!—It
went that deep!

They brought Chivv's mother back again. It took four of them to
lift her off of the rolling-table and back into her bed. Nurse told me not
to worry and not to talk to her.

'She's alright,' she said.

Later on, Chivv's mother started saying, 'Oh, doctor, I be goin' to
die.' She said it again, and again, and again . . . Nurse came in again and
told me she was alright though. Our Mother came to see me, and wasn'r
I glad to see her. She sat on a chair beside my bed and her eyes still
rolled behind the glasses. Chivv's mother let go with another one of her

'goin' to die' shouts and Mother hit the floor like a sack of tiddies! I
was out of that bed like a jack rabbit. Nurse told me that Mother was
alright and to get back to bed.

The next day, the nurse carried me in to see the doctor. I told her I
could walk, but she still carried me. I was glad none of our lot were
watching. The doctor had a mask on his face. He asked me how I was
and said he was glad to see me. He lay me on the table. Nurse put a mask
like a big tea strainer over my nose and mouth and then the doctor held
a bottle above it. They told me to start counting . . .

I awoke with a sore droat and with a shiny spit-bowl beside my head.
Somebody had swiped my pillow while I was asleep, too, I noticed. Nurse
told me I was alright and to get back to sleep.

Our Mother didn't come again until it was time to take me home. I
expected her to arrive at two o'clock, but she didn't arrive until almost
three, and I had had a good roar in the meantime. Nurse had kept on
telling me it would be alright during the waiting period, but she hadn't
had much success. Mother had had some trouble. Vather had started his
Christmas celebrations six months too early and had arrived home
soaking wet and plastered in mud. Mother said she couldn't leave him
there like that because he was making a mess of her cocoanut matting
and she had only just scrubbed it that morning.

I couldn't get out of that hospital fast enough, even though they had
been so good to me. And that nurse . . . She was alright, she was.

When I got home among the others it was just as though I had never
been away. You know what I mean. No one to keep on looking after you
all the time. Fighting with the rest of them at tea-time to get one of the
cups with a handle-on.

I couldn't go out to play that day. Had to go to bed early, too. When
bed time arrived for the others as well, there was the same old arguing
about who had all the bed clothes. You always get that when there's
enough in a bed.

Vather shouted up to tell us that he would sort us out with his strap
if we didn't bide quiet. We tried to be quiet by playing a game of 'I spy'.
The youngest wanted to have a go, so we let him start off . . .

'I spy with my liddle eye . . . Um . . . No, not he . . . Um . . . No, not
that un, neither . . . I spy with my liddle eye, a dear little word called
"vase"!'

We had to laugh at him, didn't we?

Vather wanted to know if we wanted him to come up and see to us.
(Sounded as though there was no cider money left, to us.)

This was being at home. No one had to keep on telling me that everything was alright.

There were the other illnesses for which we didn't have to go to hospital. Some the doctor would tend to. Some the District Nurse used to see to, and Our Mother had to deal with the others.

There was the rickets, of course, and this was dealt with by the high protein from the snails. I also had pneumonia and convulsion fits as a babb. Both were quite common. So was diptheria and scarlet fever and the sufferers had to go into the Isolation Hospital up behind Weary All on the Roman Way. These two complaints and leprosy were about the only illnesses our family *didn't* have! I can faintly remember having mumps . . . Measles came later, and they were easy. Our family never seemed to do anything together, apart from whooping cough and impetigo. (Or was it 'invataggo' as we used to call it?)

The District Nurse used to come to our house to treat our sores when the impetigo epidemic hit us. She would sit us down and rip off the dry dressings. 'It was the only way,' she would tell us and we got very little consolation from that little bit of information. She also used to paint some blue stuff on the open sores as well. I can't remember if it was called 'gentian violet' or 'blue unction'. They sound summat the same, don't they?

The whooping cough episode remains vividly in my mind. Cough, cough, cough, cough! it was. We coughed until we ran out of breath, or until we 'urged'. Mother would make us sit in chairs around a large Nuttal's Mintoes tin which was full of tar. She would then place a red hot poker in the tin and throw a blanket over the lot of us so that we could get full benefit of the fumes.

Did it work? Well, let's put it this way—none of us died, or suffered from weak hearts, or respiratory problems afterwards.

By the time we had got over that little lot I don't think there was another germ that dared to look at us. We played in the yards of the skin factories, the sewerage farm, and the rubbish dump with very little or no complaints, apart from the odd flea and a few lice. Fleas and lice are nothing to be proud of, but there were a lot of them about. Most folk would never admit that they had ever had them, yet can recall the times they received the double-edged, close-toothed, nit-comb treatment.

I fell out of the window and broke my arm when I was about five years old. The doctor was called, who sat me in an armchair, asked Mother to hold me against the back of the chair, and then pulled my

arm until it was set, after which it was tied up in two wooden splints. He
did a good job of it. No x-ray, no injection—not even an aspirin. He
always did a first-class job, I'm pleased to announce.

There were mustard and hot-salt poultices for ear-ache, tooth-ache
and gumboils. These were applied to the cheek and held in place with a
scarf knotted on the top of the head. The mustard poultices were
exceptionally good. The lady down the road was looking after us while
Mother was having a new addition and she left one on my face for too
long a period. I went to sleep with it on and it took the skin off my
cheek. There were boiling-hot bread poultices for boils and carbuncles.

We would take almost anything Our Mother told us to take when
there was something wrong with us. She could be a little forceful at
times, but even she had to admit defeat when it came to our consump-
tion of castor oil and margarine. It was syrup of figs, senna pod tea, and
dandelion teas when things weren't 'going' too good. There were yellow
sulphur tablets or brimstone and treacle by the spoonful for the same
kind of thing—but with spots. Codliver oil and malt to build us up. I
liked the taste of that. I liked liquid paraffin as well. Uncoo Awffy said
it gave the dog a good coat and that was good enough for me.

There were four broken legs and three broken arms between us. There
were also busted ribs and sprains, but they were classed with the cuts,
bruises, and the stitches. You can't count them all, can you?

Apart from her two-yearly 'lie-a-bed' stints Our Mother wasn't allowed
to get ill. When the 'stints' occurred one of us would have to run across-
fields to town with an 'embalope' for the District Nurse, who would get-
down-home before the messenger in order to inform him on his arrival
that he had another baby brother. Mother had become an expert 'last
minute' judge. The District Nurse made nine of these trips in all . . .
Seven boys and a girl. The other boy took one look at his surroundings
and decided not to stay.

Mother found it hard to find the money for the medical bills, so she
joined the 'Hospiddle Club'. Threepence a week for the whole family, it
was, but she had to 'chuck in' and go back to the old way of paying. We
couldn't afford it. 'Not *every* week when nobody wasn't even ill!' It was
sixpence a time for treatment from the school dentist, and two or three
visits would cost no more than the extra pain and agony.

The Flea Bloke would come to see us at school, now and again, but I
don't think he had much-idea, though. He looked quite smart in that
white coat of his, but he couldn't have been at it for very long. He was
older than us—but not *old*. You know what I mean. You could be cheeky

to him without being rude.

He would arrive in the classroom with his white enamel tray full of jam jars, combs and brushes. He would then comb and search through our hair for lice and fleas. What he did with them when he found them, I don't know. I don't know if he ever found any on me because he would never tell us anything, you see. If he didn't, I don't think I was to blame.

I remember taking a letter to the teacher from Our Mother requesting that I be allowed to keep a home-made cap on in class because I had been playing on the skins at the factory, which resulted in my hair being cropped even closer than usual and liberally rubbed with paraffin.

Tobe's brother worked on a farm and came home covered in fleas. He had been milking a cow who regularly seemed to pick up huge batches of them from somewhere.

Our dog was always lousy (very lovable, though). Before placing the dog in the tin bath (the same bath we were bathed in and the same one in which Our Mother did her washing), a handful of special wood chips were put in the water and the juice from these chips would kill the fleas. Uncoo Awffy told me the wood chips were put in there because the fleas can't swim and, after they had climbed onto a wood chip, you poured them away! Our Mother told him that I had enough dunch ideers in my head without any help from him, thank you.

It just goes to show you though. If that Flea Bloke was looking for fleas, there were far better places to look than in a classroom!

Cheerio

I was floating some matchsticks in a puddle in the gutter outside of
Mrs Jacks when a big, black, square-looking, taxi-kind of car pulled up
outside our house. The offside back wheel came to rest on a fresh pile
of horse dung and slowly forced a brown liquid to form about its base
and then dribble and flow in fits and starts on its erratic course towards
the gutter.

I could have done with some of those toy wooden boats we had for
last Christmas, really. Pity we didn't look after things a little better—
as Mother kept on telling us.

The driver got out of the car and went around onto the path beside
the back door of the car.

But then, those ships were no good in the first place. Just bits of old
wire and cardboard stuck into some wood with a cross on the top. They
didn't even have real paint on them, not real shiny paint . . .

Another bloke got out from the back door of the car.

. . . And shiny paint wouldn't have made a lot of difference, anyroad,
because those boats had flat bottoms and wouldn't float-flat . . . Top
heavy—they kept on turning over . . . Hey, half-a-mo'!—If I had those
boats I wouldn't be playing with this puddle because it wouldn't be
deep enough. Who wants boats? As I said, they weren't no good, anyroad.

The two blokes helped Gramf out of the back of the car. They put
his arms around their shoulders . . .

'Hey, Gramf! What's the matter, Gramf?'

'Go away and play, me son,' one of the men told me.

'What's up, Gramf?'

'Oh, nothin', me dear . . . You go away and play, there's a good boy
. . .'

It was alright then . . . Gramf wasn't drunk . . .

So I continued to play . . . Funny how those tiny, chewed-up bits of
horse dung looked like lots of little logs floating on the water—like the
ones I saw in that lumberjack film up-Pictures. Hey, tell you what. If I
could get lots of matches I could play logs and lumberjacks. There were

some used matches in the bottom half of the Mansion Polish tin beside the gas stove. There would be some more matches in the candlesticks in the bedrooms.

I went in-house. Our Mother grabbed hold of me, tidied me up, and sent three of us up to Aunt Kate's up-town. Here's something—Our Aunt Kate was Our Mother's Aunt Kate as well! She lived in a council house. Our Cudge, my elder brother, liked it up there, but I wasn't so sure. Aunt Kate was old. She always looked tidy and so was her house. She talked with a quiet, clipped, Anglo-Irish voice. She looked at us with a glare through her glasses that said, 'I can handle you-three,' and did!

It wasn't until we were settled in that I realized I hadn't seen Uncoo Ern for a long time. He used to sit in a chair in the bay window with his legs resting on a padded and frilled blanket-box. I always saw him in this position because he suffered from trench-sores—large, open, weeping ulcers on his shins and I would sometimes watch Aunt Kate dress them with boracic powder and lint. He was unable to work full-time, and the only time Aunt Kate could get her eight shillings a week allowance, was when Uncoo Ern was in a hospital up-Bath for one of his many long spells of treatment.

Uncoo Ern would always peel an orange and give me two segments of it when I happened to meet him. He often said, 'Oh, well. Thank God we've got the English Empire,' which I thought was a funny thing to say—even if I did get a day's holiday on Empire Day. A blood clot from his ulcers had killed him about a year previous to my present visit. I thought he might be in the Bath hospital again and did not enquire after him.

Thank you, soldier.

Aunt Kate's oven and hobbs looked better than our'n. They had been Zebo'd-black just the same, but hers had green tiles all around the fireplace. There was a 'swing-in' and 'swing-out' sort of thing over the fire to boil the kettle. She made rice puddings in her oven and she baked big meat and vegetable pies with an egg cup turned upside down to hold the centre of the pastry up. She was a good cook. Her food was delicious. Her eating rules upset me a little, though. She made cocoanut cakes with rice paper on the bottom . . . I liked cakes, but I would seem to chew and chew, but could never seem to get it to the back of my throat in order to swallow it. A sip of tea would have been the answer, but Aunt Kate said I was to eat properly and empty my mouth first. Aunt Kate's tea was very strong and was sweetened with Nestle's Condensed Milk—

not the kind you pour. You took it from the tin with a spoon—like
treacle. ('And don't lick your spoon like that!—Where are the manners
you have been taught? . . . It is not very nice, and it isn't good manners,
it isn't!')

Aunt Kate had a small smooth-haired terrier called Gip and he loved
to sleep at the foot of our bed—under the bed clothes. We liked him
there . . . He didn't take up any of the room we needed, anyroad. She
also had a black cat called Nigger who hated everyone except Aunt
Kate. When we arrived at the house, he would stay in the backroom
under the table and would cuss, swear, and attempt to scratch anyone
who tried to befriend him. ('You will leave him alone, if you have any
sense, you will.')

Our Cousin, Nora—Aunt Kate's grow'd-up daughter, was always taking
the rise out of me. She called me 'her little rainbow' and she knew I
didn't like it.

We slept three (and the dog) to a bed. Aunt Kate brought us cups of
tea with saucers on a tray in the mornings, and two biscuits each.

The first few days, Aunt Kate would send us out shopping and, after
that, out for a walk . . . ('And you will see that you come home tidy,
you will!')

We were sent to Pictures on Saturday afternoon and, after tea, it was
out for a walk again, because 'it was good for us'.

Sunday. We didn't share the thrill of Aunt Kate's Catholic upbring-
ing, so it was walks and more walks . . . ('You will not leave the table
until the others have finished their meal!' 'I do not wish to know if you
have finished your meal, or not. You will eat it, you will!')

. . . and more walks . . . keeping tidy all the time.

On the Monday, it was different. Naturally. After dinner, we were
told to go for a walk—but we were to go *where* Aunt Kate wanted us to
go. We were then to go home . . . We were not to arrive before four
o'clock, and she would be there to see that we did not! . . . And we were
not to play Our Mother up, we weren't . . .

We were ready to go. I hadn't worn my best suit so many times all-at-
once before.

Aunt Kate's blinds were drawn . . .

('To keep the sun out, of course!')

Aunt Kate wore her black, flowered hat and the black astrakan coat . . .

('And did she not feel the cold?—Even if the sun *was* out!')

She kept the backroom locked today . . . because Nigger was in there?
I saw her unlock the door and enter the room . . . I quickly followed . . .

Nigger *was* in there . . . He was under the table . . . There was a wreath *on* the table . . .

'Is Gramf dead, Aunt Kate?'

She looked a bit on the old-fashioned-side at me . . . Funny how spectacles tend to flip folk's eyes about when they are uneasy . . .

'Yes,' she said.

'Oh,' I said . . . and, of course . . . I never saw dear old Gramf again . . .

We walked . . . Why had we been up Aunt Kate's for so long? Why hadn't we been home with Gramf? I was getting fed up with this!

'Bugger these walks!' I thought. 'Bugger all this walkin' and keepin' tidy and goin' where I've been told to go all the time!' I didn't say anything, mind. The other two would have told Our Mother.

I left the other two, who wouldn't come home with me, and arrived home at three o'clock. Aunt Kate waited for me, as promised . . . and cuddled me . . .

'OLD, is when you start sayin' the same things . . . over and over again, more often!'

The words of a dead man at fifty-seven . . .

What went wrong, Gramf? Why hadn't they given you a fair crack o' the whip?

Gone . . . Everything gone . . . Gone, were those occasional, magical, Sunday morning walks with Our Gramf . . . Gone, were the seekings of the carefully lost pennies and halfpennies under the kitchen table on a pay night . . .

Those walks . . . We often went to the same places on our own—but you *saw* more with Gramf! Catkins, sticky-buds, and falling leaves. All had a meaning when you saw them with Gramf—a special meaning. Butterflies became different kinds of butterflies who's only aim in life *wasn't* to eat our cabbages and live their lives in jam jars with a holed-paper cover. Wild birds were something to be enjoyed. 'Don't never steal a robin's egg or thy fingers will grow crooked' . . . and don't *steal* birds eggs, anyroad, because 'it ain't a very nice thing to do—not if you like to watch um fly about and sing to us so pretty.'

'That gert elum tree. He must have took about two-hunderd-year to grow that big.'

Those memorable walks were shared by others, but belonged only to me.

The preparation that was needed! It was on these Sunday mornings that Gramf's Indian Army training used to force its way into existence. Our boots had to be polished to go on these magical trips. Your jersey could be worn in holes at the 'olbows'. Your trousers may have needed another major re-seating job. Maybe there was no possible way to keep your stockings pulled up—but those boots had to be polished—without leaving marks on the stockings!

'Take um off and do um properly, me dear . . . Take pride in thyself.'

Take them off?—But he might go before I could get them back on again. I could tie those laces up, but my nail-bitten fingers could never 'undo' them. Neither could anyone else, for that matter! A piece of paper inserted between the top of the boot and the stocking was the answer. Boots were bigger than shoes when it came to polishing, but it had to be boots for us. Shoes were out of the question. True, they were easier to get on and off, but they showed the holes in the heels of the stockings. Yes, I know . . . Slide the hole beneath the heel and fold the toe of the stocking under your toes, but this could make walking very uncomfortable. And there was the operation of pulling one's stockings up. With the toes folded under, this had to be done twice as often and twice as hard. The stockings would stretch and continue to sink down to the tops of one's boots more rapidly.

I experimented. I would pull them up and hold my breath as I walked. It didn't work. I tried again. Newspaper shin-guards. I could always say I was going to play football afterwards, if asked. I was proud of the result.

With Gramf—no matter where we went—whatever direction we took— Main Road, Back Roads, across fields, or up over the hills, we would eventually arrive at the railway line. Gramf loved his railway . . .

There was the time we were walking across a field . . . The grass had been grazed short, and the cows hadn't left the field long-ago-enough for the hands to go 'turd bashing', when this cow-dog suddenly appeared and tore into our'n like a good-un. The cow-dog yiped and beat a hasty retreat with a three-cornered rent in its side. The farmer was very wild and he didn't half carry on at us!

'Sorry about thy dog, Leonard,' said Gramf, 'but he *did* jump on our'n.'

'You'm sorry?' said Varmer, and so be I!—You haven't got no business on my land, anyroad!'

'Thy land?' said Gramf . . . 'Leonard. It do seem to I that the only time I've got any land to call me own is when there's a war on to fight for it. I seem to remember thee wavin' the lads off to war from the door of the Red Lion. Oh, I know *somebody* had to stay behind and look after the land, Leonard, but thee tell I—I don't s'pose you've happened to see my little bit of land anywhere, have 'ee? It wouldn't be a big bit. Just enough to stand on with both feet for about half a minute!'

We continued our walk across the field. The cow-dog circled and closed in again . . . Would he never learn? . . . Oh, well . . .

'Take that dog of thine in hand, me dear,' said Gramf. 'That's how wars do get started.'

Elm trees . . . The gentle giants. They looked so big . . . so beautiful . . . so many . . . They looked like 'forever'.

Lead, Kindly Light

You have all heard of the Glastonbury Carnival, no doubt? Don't know why I bothered to ask really, because I'm sure *everybody in the world* must know that it takes place in the freezing-cold days of November— when the human friezes freeze to immobility as much as their shivering bodies will allow.

'Oh, she do look lovely, don't she—but she do look shrammed to death with the cold, don't she?'

It takes a special kind of person to participate in this carnival—with built-in determination and sources of inner warmth, a sense of humour, and a pride in hard-won certificates, because they have never competed for the money, I'm sure.

As times have changed the floats have become bigger, better, longer, brighter, more mechanized, illuminated, commercial, and more abundant.

My first carnivals were when there was an equal amount of horses and carts and 'they new lorries', and were something I watched with awe and delight. I can remember trying to force myself back onto the crowded pavement when I was attacked by King Kong, who lunged from one side of the narrow road to the other as he attempted to grab the unsuspecting children on the kerb and my life was saved by the timely intervention of King Kong's keepers as they jerked him away on his chains. This was also the night I did not have to be reminded to 'keep in close' and 'not get in the way of the wheels, or else I'd be sorry'. They were mad, hilarious nights. The pride and joy of the participants combined with joy and delight of the onlookers made them times to remember with deep warmth and affection. I cannot remember ever feeling cold as I watched those early parades.

The drunks shouted and were shouted down by the indignant crowds as they clapped and cheered the brightly lit procession passing on the usually dim gas-lit streets.

I always seemed to be in danger of getting trampled to death by the men who walked the gutters clink-clink-clinking their wooden collection boxes with the carnival cards attached to them. The printer's ink was usually still wet on them. I had first-class knowledge of this because they approached me face high from out of nowhere and I would turn panic-stricken to whoever happened to be with me because I never had anything to put in the box.

The lucky folk who watched indoors from their upstairs windows were not ignored by the collectors. Some had long poles with a sort of wind-sock attached to them and the upstairs folk would place their offerings in the open-mouthed end and it would slide down inside to the collector's hand.

Those lucky upstairs folk who didn't have to come out for the carnival! One day, I decided, I shall have one of those houses, and I shall sit at the window to watch the carnival with fish and chips and meat pies and bottles of Tizer and a couple of bottles of Trask's lime-ade and I would have my piles of coppers placed ready on the window sill for when the collectors came along.

Those poor upstairs folk. They most probably felt a little persecuted, because one coin did not seem to have the weight to force itself down the coarse bunting sock and thus necessitated the presentation of more than one coin. The wooden-box-collector could see what you offered, but the sock-collector could only guess by the 'chink' of the coppers as they slid down the sock—and this sound was observed by most in the crowd above the din of the carnival. There were occasions when a lighted cigarette end was included with the coppers and the screams, shouts, oaths, threats and shaken fists were all absorbed in the atmosphere of Carnival Night.

Some of the local louts would save their fireworks for this night and seemed to make spaces on the pavements where tightly packed folk had been unable to move a little before. More shouting, screams, oaths and threats . . .

'Hey! Mind you don't make they horses shy! You dunch young fools, you!'

'If I can get me hands on they, I'll make um laugh, I will—t'other side of their faces!'

Taking part in the procession, and unnoticed by all, were the torch bearers. These were recruited from the ranks of the children and youths just before the commencement of the parade. They didn't dress up. They were paid a tanner (2½p) to carry a single, and a bob (5p) for a double, and they would then be placed in ones and twos between the floats where they would remain for the duration of the carnival.

The torches were a sort of large round can fixed on the end of a long broom handle. The wick emerged from the top of the can and this was lit by the Torch Lighter after he placed you in position, and *his* torch always seemed to go out just before the procession commenced. The torches were very heavy and, judging by the dark liquid that dribbled down the handle of the first torch I carried, they burnt a mixture of 'parafeen', creosote and tar. They lasted for hours and could not be blown out.

, I had never wanted to take part in the carnival until I decided I was big enough to carry a torch—which was just after I found out there was a tanner on the end of it. I couldn't have started on a worst year of my career as a torch bearer. My confidence took a knock from the very first moment.

'Thee sure you'm strong enough to carry one of these torches, me son?' Torch Lighter enquired of me with an expression of concern which tended to cut me down to half of my already inadequate size.

'Yes, I'm *strong*, mister,' I replied.

'Don't look as though there's enough of thee to make a good stew,' Torch Lighter observed. 'Still, I'll take a chance on thee, but bemember, mind, if you don't do the lot, you don't get paid. Alright?'

'Alright, Mister. Thanks, mister.'

I hadn't tested the weight of those torches and they weighed twice as much as I had imagined.

The night was cold and there was a mad, screaming east wind which seemed to be trying to tear the clothes from my body. The glamour of the carnival was already beginning to wane a little. 'I'll bet my light gets "dowted" out,' I thought to myself. I was stationed between a horse and waggon and an old lorry. The waggon was in front of me and along the apron on the side of it were the crudely painted words 'Farmyard Frolics', which I considered to be a rather naughty title at the time. I looked wistfully at the two men sat in their lorry behind me. They looked so comfortable sat there, and they laughed and joked with one another as they tucked a sort of canvas apron about themselves in their windowless, windscreen-less cab. 'If they hung it all-round like a curtain, they could cut two holes in it to see through and then they'd be more lovely and warm in there,' I thought.

I waited for the show to start . . . The torch pressed tightly into my shoulder, so I transferred it to the other. I had never known my hands so cold. The wooden handle of the torch seemed to be made of ice-cold, slippery steel.

My thin jacket was down to its last button and the wind played havoc with the lower unbuttoned half. It seemed to go around and around in-

side like a torrent of ice-cold river water. I contemplated tying my scarf
about my waist, but that would have meant getting a cold throat and
chest and they had to be protected at all cost because there was so much
trouble with them.

If only my stockings would stay up. I had tried pulling them up over
my knees, but they had refused to stay there even whilst I was standing
still. I wished I was wearing those grey and blue ones with the 'laskit'
garter made into them. They used to stay up, but I'd worn them out
last summer.

—And these trousers didn't help much! Never had such a bad pair
of trousers, I hadn't! They were a pair of hand-me-downs of my elder
brother and they were very short and tight. They sort of made me want
to walk on tippy-toe all the time. Why couldn't he be like me?—When I
was finished with a pair of trousers, they were well and truly finished, I
can tell you. My thoughts travelled back to the pair of 'cordroys' I had
had a couple of years earlier. Now, they were a real pair of trousers. They
were far too big for me. The bottoms of the legs came well below my
knees. ('They'll keep thy legs warm and thy knees clean for a change!'—
in the summer time?). The tops came so high up my chest that I was
unable to shorten my 'bracers' enough to be effective—Another inch and
I could have pinned them over my shoulders.

This torch was making my other shoulder ache, now . . . Wish I had
those trousers now . . . They'd be so much warmer . . . They must have
been a pair of men's cut off below the knee . . . Couldn't have been a
pair of Vather's because he only wore grey flannels. Remember the pair
he wore and wore, and Our Mother sewed and patched the knees until
there was nothing but patches and lumps to patch up and he wouldn't
change them? . . . Probably because it was too big a job to get the
bracers off, because the buttons had been long gone and he'd fixed
them with matchsticks and shoe rivets . . . Anyroad, Our Mother cut
them off below the knees while he was sleeping it off one Sunday afternoon and I can remember the laugh we had when he got up and put
them on again.

Those old cordroys of mine . . . They were too hot in the summer
and when I took my jersey and shirt off to play I had to tie an old jersey
tie about my waist and then turn about six inches of trousers down
over. That might not sound like a lot, but it is when you're only about
three-foot-six. They were ever so hot and uncomfortable like that, but
I bet they'd be ever so warm now . . .

I didn't have a hanky with me again, and my nose started to run twice as much as soon as I realized this . . .

The men in the lorry were sipping hot cups of tea from a flask. I
could hear them. They laughed as the wind gusted in under to billow
their canvas apron . . . I would have brought some bread and cheese as
well, if I'd been one of them . . .

We started to move at last . . . Not very fast . . . Why didn't they get
a move on and then slow down a bit when we got to the important bits
down in town? I might see somebody I knew down there, and they'd
be able to see me carrying a torch in the carnival . . . The inner glow of
this thought was gutted like a candle flame as we turned a corner and
the wind immediately seemed to sense I was a little more vulnerable on
this stretch of road which was open to the farmland on one side. I'll bet
it would be warmer down town . . . It couldn't be colder—I was noddled!

'Hey, Young'un!'

I was suddenly brought back to my duties by a man who was stood
on the waggon in front. He looked wild about something.

'Yes, mister?' I asked.

'Don't get so close to our float. We've got straw up here and there's
sparks flyin' off thiick torch of thine . . . We shall go up in a flash of
smoke if you ain't more careful.'

'Alright. Sorry, Mister.'

Well, I *had* to be nice, didn't I? I was new to the job, and I wanted
that sixpence so much . . . I *had* to be humble about it all, didn't I?

'Slow up. Slow up!' Torch Lighter shouted. 'We want folk to *see* us!
. . . Goin' like a flash o' lightnin' you-lot be . . . More like the Charge of
the Light Brigade than a carnival, 'tis . . . Slow up!'

I eyed his 'wooden bottle' of cider about his waist. His face looked
flush enough to be warm. He'd make the carnival last all night if he had
his way.

'Hey! I said slow up at the back there!'

Ordinary little men with a little bit of extra power. Like the time
they put that nice little man on the door down Picture House. He was
never the same bloke while he had that job . . . Made our lives a misery
with all his orders and shouting and telling we kids what to do all the
time . . .

'Hey! Didn't thiick bloke tell thee to slow up? Get back a bit or you'll
have we on fire!'

Mouthy sod! . . . Dressed up like Poor Old Farmer . . . We all know he
ain't no farmer . . . They haven't got no time to do summat for nothin'
. . . They'd rent the horse and waggon out for a profit, but they wouldn't

do nothin' like this . . . Don't recognize the horse, neither . . . Must be a foreigner from somewhere outside town . . .

'Have I got to tell thee again? Keep back from my float, else we shall all be warmed up with no thanks to thee!'

His float now, is it? . . . Looks more like a waggon to me . . . And with they hay racks up at both ends he still don't look like a hay wain . . . Hay wains have got sides on um with raives out over the wheels . . . Hay wains ain't flat-bedded waggons with hay racks fitted on each end . . . And he don't belong to thee anyroad, Loud Mouth! I'll bet Poor Old Farmer haven't even got time to drag his-self away from his comfortable fire and his cider jar to come out here and see us freeze to death.

Oh, God, I was so cold. The wind was getting worse than ever. Hey, hang on a minute. What was I thinking of? Here was I—freezing to death —and I had a flame on the top-end of this torch! I must be dunch! I slowly let the handle slide through my hands . . . No, I couldn't feel any extra warmth yet . . . A little lower then . . . Now, I wonder if I can hold it one-handed?

'Hey, Useless!' Farmer Fake shouted. 'What be 'ee tryin' to do now?— Climb up the bloody thing?'

Any more lip from him and I'll burn his breeches . . .

'Any more of thy blimmin' nonsense and I'll see the bloke about thee, I will!—And keep clear of our float. I shan't tell thee again!'

A woman stepped from the crowd with a flask . . . and gave it to the men in the lorry. They returned the empty flask with a few cheerful words and a laugh or two . . . Pity she hadn't thought of bringing some sandwiches . . . I'm sure they would have enjoyed them as well!

They honked their horn at me to let me know I was falling back too far. I wondered if they'd stop drinking tea if they happened to run over me . . . I wondered if they'd stop!

'Hullo, Aunty Vere.'

'Oh, hullo, me dear . . . Oh, you look scrammed to death, you do . . . And just look at the state of thee! What's all that black stuff?'

I was so cold I hadn't noticed. The browny-black liquid had oozed down the handle and my face, neck, shoulders and hands were covered in it.

'Take him on home, missus,' cried Farmer Fake. 'Thiick young'un's a soddin' nuisance!'

'I'll give thee "soddin' nuisance" if I come up there long with thee!' flared Aunt Vere. 'Just thee keep a civil tongue in thy head!'

The crowd cheered and Farmer Fake quickly found someone else to

talk to on the other side of the street. Aunt Vere's sixteen stone and a
good quick temper were a joy to watch when she was on your side.

It was just after this we turned into Northload Street: 'Narlit Street'
or just 'Narlit' to us. This was one of the poorer residential areas. Narlit
folk were different from Beckery folk, but we were the *same*. It was a
poor, rundown, dilapidated area. The walls of the houses bulged and
the cracked plaster was falling onto the pavements. Some of the cracked
windows were covered inside with cardboard and the curtains looked too
tired to move. The front doors were permanently open and flagstones
covered the floors through the passages. There were worse residences
than these, though. Beside the fish and chip shop was an alley containing a row of small shabby cottages with their outside taps. On the other
side of the alley was the communal, non-segregated toilets. The passage
entrance was so narrow that it was completely blocked when a certain
fat lady resident paused there for her haporth of news. Folk referred to
this place as 'Down the Drain'.

Narlit had a name for poverty, drunkenness and violence. There were
four very busy pubs in the first 150 yards. Gypsies wishing to sell their
horses would race them up and down the crowded street on Market
Day. There were fights and drunken brawls and folk still talk of the
knife fights that used to be.

I sighed with relief as we entered the street. It was almost like going
to church. The wind still gusted, but at least we were sheltered from
the steady icy blast. The crowds were thicker here, too—most probably
because the road was so much narrower and the extra shelter it provided.

God, didn't those fish and chips smell good? Hot, fatty chips . . .
almost too hot to pick up with the fingers . . . Fried, battered fish which
gusted a cloud of steam and heat as you broke it open . . . I wonder
why their salt and vinegar always taste so much better than ours? And
they never taste the same once they have been removed from the newspaper, do they? A woman stepped out from the crowd and handed two
newspaper bundles of fish and chips to the men in the lorry—No wonder
they didn't want any sandwiches! Now I suppose I'd have to smell them
and listen to them smacking their chops and licking their fingers all along
the street . . .

'Hey, young'un! Haven't I told thee?—Art thee dunch, or summat?'
Farmer Fake was at it again.

'Leave the young'un be!' shouted a voice from the crowd. 'You
ain't out-in-field now, you know!'

This did not mean that I had found support and protection from the crowd. If two folk were arguing and one of them happened to be a farmer—right or wrong, symbolic or 'for real'—the crowd would be on the other man's side. Still, off-handed, misguided support was better than nothing.

'Ah,' I enjoined, 'Shut thy mouth or I'll get Our Aunty Vere for thee!'

There were cheers from the crowd.

'That's right, young'un. Thee tell un!'

About half-way along Narlit, four big lads appeared beside me.

'Thiick torch is too heavy for thee. I'll carry it for thee and we can go "snicks".'

I had been warned of these kind offers. They would take it from me by force, if need be, and I could whistle for my share when they had collected the money.

'I'm alright, thanks,' I replied.

'We said we'd help thee, didn't us?' the intruders insisted as they grabbed hold of the torch. I could see I was on to a hiding to nothing here. I was cold. I was tired, but there was that nasty uneasy feeling about giving in without fighting.

'Leave un be, young'un. He's alright. He's me mate.'

Tobe had come to the rescue. Another couple of ticks and his elder brother and company would have completed their take-over bid. And as if I didn't have enough trouble already . . . Farmer Fake was complaining to Torch Lighter . . .

'Nearly caught we alight about half-a-dozen times already, he have . . . He's cheeky and he won't do like you've been tellin' us to do—and you've got a hard job, I know . . . He's spoilin' my carnival, he is . . . ' *HIS* carnival?! If things go on like this they'll be marryin' he off to the Carnival Queen and then they'll be makin' him King of Glastonbury, if we don't watch out . . .

I squirmed in silence whilst Farmer Fake leered at me as Torch Lighter gave his verdict in buttered-up, cider-skimmished words.

'Any more trouble from thee—and I've had a night of it, I can tell thee' (I could see that) . . . 'and you'll be out of the carnival on your ear-hole . . .'

That's justice for you . . . Carnival?—It was more like a blimmin' battle ground!

The parade rounded the corner,—straight into the teeth of the gale which had been saving up all its puff for the moment I came out of Narlit. I admit I was wrong . . . I said it couldn't have been any colder,

but it could be, and it was doing it now! The wind struck me so fiercely
and so cold I could hardly catch my breath. I kept my head down,
pressing my chin tightly into my scarf, and my lips seemed to be almost
torn from my gritted teeth. The lorry parped and honked as my huddled,
aching back hopefully attempted to drag some warmth from the radiator. Was it my imagination, or did that horn really belch fumes of
fish and chips at me? After all, they say that a man dying of starvation
always dreams of fish and chips, don't they?

Farmer Fake was shouting again from somewhere up in front. I lifted
my head to face the biting wind to see what in the hell was wrong with
him this time. I couldn't be too close to him because I was still trying
to get a warm from the lorry . . . Shouting here . . . shouting there . . .
Honk-honk here . . . Parp-parp there . . . Too far up. Too far back . . .
What did he want me to do?—Get run over?

Farmer Fake was down in the gutter stamping and jumping up and
down on a blazing pile of wood-straw. (Didn't even know where to find
the real stuff, I don't expect.) His feet were doing a good job, but his
oaths and hot air seemed to be doing an equally good job of keeping
them alight. The crowd joined in and fag packets, fish and chip paper,
and lighted fag ends were added to help smother the flames. There were
the usual oaths, shouts, screams and shrieks of laughter. The lorry had
come to a halt and I leant against the radiator to enjoy my ringside
view. I wasn't going to help him. He didn't want me near his precious
float. Well, he said this would happen, didn't he? Said it over and over
again, he had. He'd been pointing the black stick at himself all night,
hadn't he? Couldn't have happened to better bloke, neither.

Tobe stood beside me grinning like a young spring bull who had been
turned out with a herd of young cows for the first time in his life.

'You didn't do that, did 'ee?' he asked with unabashed admiration.

Couldn't he see the wind was blowing the wrong way? No, he couldn't.
He didn't want to, and I bet everybody else was thinking the same thing.

They must have had a private telephone line to the nearest pub, because
Torch Lighter was trying to force his way through the crowd. His sense of
duty and urgency only seemed to stir the crowd to more amusing thoughts.

'Let I droo! Let I droo!' he shouted, and the crowd pressed more
tightly about him.

'Come on, you-lot, let I droo!—'Tis me job, and I've got to see to it,
see?'

'Sorry, Gilby . . . Can't let thee droo . . . One puff of thy breath on
they embers and half of Glastonbury will be gone . . .'

'EMBERS?' enquired the astounded Torch Lighter.

'Oh, ah . . . Embers it is, me son . . . Horse, cart . . . and the poor folk went off like a shower o' damp squibs, they did' . . .

'Copper's comin',' said Tobe.

I could see his helmet threading its way through the crowd. Doctor Morse, the Narlit knackerman, pressed a penny into my hand.

'Better shove off, me son . . . Best laugh I've had all night.'

He believed it too! I had already had a sample of Torch Lighter's justice. Farmer Fake had been bad enough before he'd gotten himself into this bad temper. The last of my hopes and dreams faded with the final stamp of Farmer Fake's boot. He commenced to curse, shout, glare, and shake his fist in my direction.

'I'll soon put the brakes on he, me son,' Doctor promised.

'Finish off for me, Tobe?' I asked. 'Snicks?'

'Of course. Snicks.'

Our hands touched on the sticky broom handle . . .

'Promise?' I asked.

'Jonick' . . . and that was good enough for me.

Not for me the complicated and obstructive problems of the Copper and Torch Lighter. I followed the narrow, irregular passageway through the crowd to the sanctity of Narlit once more. I bought a pennuth of chips and took them home to share with Our Mother because I was in such a dirty mess. The chips were cold by the time I got home. We put them in the oven to warm up whilst the bread and butter was cut. There weren't many chips for a penny, but quite enough for a couple of chip sandwiches.

Tobe and I were in school doing some book-binding on the Monday morning when I broached the subject of my threepence. He didn't have it because his elder brother had taken the lot from him. After all, he'd been the one to sound me out in the first place, hadn't he? I believed Tobe. I thumped Tobe, which didn't do me a lot of good, so I thumped him again. He picked up the paper-cutting knife to warn me off, and I was so wild I didn't see it in time and hit it. He got caned for it and I got my first two stitches. Good job we were mates, otherwise there could have been some bad blood there. One of my younger brothers kicked the scar open again just after I had had the stitches taken out. I can't remember what for . . .

The problem of torch bearing was tackled in an entirely different way

the following year. There was no wind and it was quite a good night for
November.

Tobe and I collected two torches. We hid these in a farm lane and,
after donning our overcoats and caps (I'd borrowed Vather's), we re-
joined the ranks and 'drew' another two torches. We joined the queue
to be placed in our positions. Torch Lighter was a different man this
year. This one wore a navy blue suit and I disliked him more than last
year's model. Tobe was shunted off on his own. It looked as though I
was going to have a grey cart-horse walking behind me this time with a
Kentucky Minstrel walking in front of me.

'Hello, Ray,' said the minstrel. 'What do you think?'

I recognized the voice. It was Lovely Leslie, the Teacher's Pet. I
wasn't lighting the way for him, not for anybody, so I went back to
talk to Tobe whilst they placed the next one in line in my place.

'Lovely Lez is up there, all dolled up like a marmalade bloke with a
banjo,' I informed Tobe with indignation.

'Pity,' he replied, "cos Our Young'un's lookin' for a cheap pianner-
cardion.'

Torch Lighter positioned me in front of a brown mare with three
Spanish accordion-players in front of me. They looked quite smiggit all
dressed up in their black, white and silver, bolero jackets and flared
trousers. The 'Imperial Accordion Band' . . .

'Hullo, hullo, hullo, and what have we got here then?' I exclaimed
with no small measure of pride. Uncoo Awffy glared at me from beneath
his tasselled, cardboard flat hat like a rat in a bundle of straw.

'Hang on a minute, Zess. I ain't havin' *he* there. He'll have we burnt
to a frazzle before we can get down town!'

. . . and I was moved from there to a position between a lorry from
Snow's sawmills and another which kept its load a carefully guarded
secret from me. Nothing happened all the way around. I didn't see anyone who was interested in me, and Our Aunty Vere was at home with
my new cousin, Maggie. Well, the Narlit Nudgers did pay me a call, but
I just said, 'Shove off. Check up with Tobe.'

As the torch bearers arrived at the end of the carnival, they would
approach Torch Lighter, who would plunge the lighted torches into a
tub of water. This not only extinguished the light but prevented the
more devious from relighting them and collecting another tanner. Tobe
and I collected our spare torches, lit them, shed our overcoats and caps
and collected our extra sixpences. (His elder brother had told him how
to do this.)

'Alright this time?' he asked me as we re-donned our overcoats.

'Ah, 'tis,' I replied, 'as long as there's none of thy relations about!'

Now that was a thought. Where were his relations? A crowd of folk crowded around some crying damsel in distress. We pushed through the crowd and there was Lovely Lez crying as though his heart would break.

'I know who he is,' I told the crowd. 'What's the matter Lez?'

'A rough bunch of blokes pushed me about and stole my daddy's ukulele!' he sobbed, with tears making a mess of his burnt cork countenance.

'His *what*?'

'Ukulele,' Tobe informed me, 'A sort of a banjo, 'tis.'

'Well, don't worry too much, Lez,' I said, 'I 'spect you'll get it back when they get fed up with it.'

Tobe and I walked townwards . . . I expect they climbed the twelve-foot Abbey Wall by the telegraph post, went down across Abbey Park, crossed over to Fairfield, through Paradise Allotments, and back into Narlit from the other end. No one would have seen or noticed them on Carnival Night.

'I thought you said he were lookin' for a pianner-cardion,' I said to Tobe without looking at him.

'Who were?' he replied without looking at me . . . And we both had a good laugh.

Tor Fair Days

It is said that Tor Fair was held for two to three hundred years before Henry I granted the Charter to the Monastery in 1127. That's going back a bit, isn't it?—They've changed the swings since then, mind.

It was called Tor Fair because it was held in the fields nigh to the bottom of the Glastonbury Tor. In my time, Tor Fair has always been held in the Fairfield which is situated beside the Main Road on the outskirts of town. (T'was a good job they had a field called that, because it came in handy, didn't it?)

We always had a holiday on this day.

About a week before the great day, our fair would arrive in dribs and drabs and huge, slow-moving steam engines would tow two massive caravans loaded to the sky with equipment. Should I see some of this arrive on my way to school, I would proclaim to the others in the playground with no small measure of importance ...

'Hodges's have come. Saw them down be Station!'

... only to find the wind extracted from my sails with one great suck ...

'Hill's came down past our place at eleben o'clock, last night.'

(Hill's were bigger and better ... Why didn't they all come the Station way?)

No operation of assembly was ever more closely supervised by so many young experts—experts who shunned the thoughts of Unions and would willingly assist any operation with no thought of reward. This did not include the frequent trips to the nearby Railway Hotel to replenish the stocks of Usher's Home Brewed for which the princely sum of one halfpenny per trip was gratefully accepted. The same boy was responsible to the same group of fair workers each time.

There was also the trip to the fish and chip shop just around the corner, opposite the Police Station. ('And a haporth of scrump, please, Missiz Elstin.') Should the queue be too long there was the mad scamper to the other fish and chip shop, on-up-to-Cross and down Narlit. Here, a kid's pennuth of chips was worth tuppence down-t'other-way and, if the order was big enough, Mr and Mrs Knight would throw in the scrump for nothing. (I wonder what happened to those fried apple and potato scollops we used to buy?)

The amusements and stalls would settle in the lower half of the field. The top half was reserved for the sale of beasts and for the use of the 'cheap jacks'. The cost of a pair of trousers or some curtain material would cost less, but the bone-handled pocket knife—so handy for cutting your bread anc cheese could cost the shop price—or more, if you were careless. They also sold half-crowns in envelopes, if you were lucky.

The big day would be on a Monday. What a land of make-believe!

We would depart from home early in the morning with threepence to last each of us for the whole day. One had to be shrewd. Was it to be a penny ride on the Roundabouts or the 'Nose Ark'. What about a half-penny go on the manual swings with the multi-coloured, fluffy-handled ropes to pull on? It didn't matter when the money had been well spent. I could hop on the step on the whirling roundabouts if I was broke and take my chance of being literally thrown off if the money-collector caught me. Golden, green and red decorative horses, cockerels and ostriches . . . How they used to whizz by . . .

There was more coppers to be earnt from the ever-thirsty fair blokes. I had an advantage over the other 'runners'. Vather was well known to the landlord and, as his son, I could deliver on non-Tor Fair days when the pubs were closed.

There were the games of hide-and-seek and 'You're it' in a mad scrabble among the other folk. It cost nothing. The stalls and sideshows offering their wares and challenges could cost a little more.

It was hard to remove a cocoa nut from its sawdust-filled cup even when one scored a direct hit. We removed them far more easily from the sack at the back of the stall whilst another two of us would fight one another beside the man and his box of wooden balls.

The sweets and brandy-snap stalls were crowded . . . so close to those at the front of the counter . . . The others would stand in a group to one side. Should the stall-holder shout, they would split to allow the culprit to make his getaway. The occasion never arose.

Home quickly for dinner and rush back again in case we miss something.

There was a man with a small portable stall which he held with one hand as it balanced on its one solitary leg. It had a table skittle stand upon it with one skittle. The sides of the stall was open to the front and to the man holding it. The other two sides were fenced in with felt covered boards on which prizes of watches and trinkets were attached. He would

let you have a free go to show you how easy it was and no matter how
bad or clumsy you were—you would hit the skittle down. You paid your
penny . . . and missed . . . every time!

It was after he had supped his dinner at the Railway Inn on a day
when the wind scuffed-roughly, that the Skittle Bloke staggered, tottered,
and lurched with his stall in full sail, to finally flounder on the shores of
the Noah's Ark beneath the waves and cheers of the awaiting children.

One of the watches had no innards in it. The other would always stop
at half-past Micky Mouse's left foot. I didn't have either of them because
Our Mother would have wanted to know where I had gotten it from . . .
and blokes didn't wear beads, did they?

One sideshow in particular was worthy of my curious attention. They
would all come out-front like a circus to do their little bits on a platform
. . . Handstands . . . Eat a sugar 'clay' pipe . . . and they had this pelican
with out-stretched wings that never moved. It was stuffed, of course. I
knew this because I had watched it closely several times. I moved in
close . . . The Barker was bawling his head off . . . The pelican's wing
towered above me . . . I reached up and gave it a tap—and the blimmin'
bird almost bit my hand off!

The only time Vather went out with Our Mother was on Tor Fair days.
He didn't do it every year. He usually left her to go to the pubs. There
were hundreds of people in the fairground. It was the devil's own job
trying to find one particular person. It was so crowded it was difficult
to move from one place to another. Now, just add those odds up. Our
Mother and Vather were a couple of feet from me when I tapped that
pelican! I had to spend the rest of the evening hanging onto the handle
of the pram. ('And don't you dare let go, mind!') I went home early
when Mother did . . . and wondered where Vather had gone.

On another occasion we were late getting home. We should have been
home by six o'clock if we didn't see Mother and Vather and they hadn't
turned up. We arrived home at seven o'clock and the young'uns had been
briefed.

Vather waited at the front door—muffler-dressed, ready for the pubs
with his belt held at the ready in one hand. We opened the front gate
. . . paused . . . closed the front gate . . . paused . . . and walked towards
the front door . . . At the half-way mark I shouted, 'Now!' We charged
towards the doorway and crowded against Vather to prevent him from
getting a good swing. We immediately broke away from him and rushed
upstairs to where we were going to be sent without any tea or supper,
anyroad.

We tore into the bedroom with Vather close at heel. There were two beds in that room, and over, under, or around was the order for the day —with everyone for himself. We could move with the best. Put the fear of God into us—and we could do better. We yiped with every close miss . . . Vather was furious and in his temper he knocked the carbuncle on his wrist against the underside of the bed after missing us with another frenzied swing. He retired, turning the air blue with the language we had come to regard as true affection . . . and we went to sleep to sounds of rattling, rumbling, empty bellies . . . and the sound of Tor Fair in the wailing distance.

And what of the music of Tor Fair? Have you ever *really* listened to it? Most comes from the loud-speaker'd records of the 78.R variety . . . It helps. But did you ever listen to the roundabouts playing the same old tunes in the same old, old way on the same old hirdy-girdies? Watch the little wooden man rat-a-tat his kiddle-drum . . . Watch the drums, cymbals and horns play a tune without aid . . . What?—You can't abide the circular motion?—Then walk around beside it! How loud it is . . . The noise, and now the blast! . . . and back to the sound that just deafens. Talk about it, talk to it! . . . Shout over it . . . Scream at it!

But listen, listen to it, damn your unseeing ears—listen! . . . and it will softly tell you that it—and all things—were young once upon a time.

Shut thy Mouth!

Fear and respect were almost one and the same thing to me.

I had to 'fear the Lord my God', which was never explained to me, and a parrot-fashion form of remembrance was all that was required.

If I stepped out of line, there was always Our Mother or Vather to set me back on the right road again with the usual amount of gentle persuasion.

The police were always at hand when I had slipped up. They could send me to jail or Borstal if I did anything really bad.

The headmaster and his staff dealt out their corporal punishment with an air of boredom. This not only applied to school matters but to my behaviour outside as well! If someone reported me for cheek or bad language there was no trial and 'Sir' would come down on me like a ton of bricks.

Even the vicar carried his share of power. He never corrected you with a cuff but he would pass his report onto the headmaster to adjust this slight weakness of his character.

Shopkeepers, in their own little kingdoms, treated me with the contempt I had learnt to deserve even when I entered their shops as a customer.

They were all forms of authority and there seemed to be an invisible barrier between them and the folk. Attempts to break that barrier from our side in order to better one's self was regarded as 'snotty, or toffee nosed', 'too big for their boots', or 'swanky'.

I was always quick to observe and take advantage when the barrier was broken from the other side.

The headmaster used to smile when he played cricket with the boys in the playground. Was he at his happiest when he played cricket with them? He would never play with me because I didn't like cricket. I know I know who swiped the school cricket bat, though.

A policeman used to come down Station Road in his best suit to go courting. We would grin and leer at him. Hands held behind our backs . . . 'Hul-lo?' . . . Knees bend and straighten up again . . . 'And what have we got here then?' He would say nothing—but I bet he wished we were hardened criminals.

Mr and Mrs Shopkeeper came on a Sunday School outing with us. They tried to spend their time with the Sunday school teachers, but the teachers had a lot of organizing to do and couldn't pay much attention to them. Their conversations with the folk tended to fade after the initial greetings. I accepted the ice cream they offered me and got blamed when their son got lost on the sands. I didn't even like the young'un—let alone play with him!

Our vicar liked his drop of cider. He also drove an old Ford or Austin. We once found him when he was the worse for wear in his car and had been forced to park beside the road. He wondered if we would care to direct him homewards? We did ... Three inside, one on each running-board, one on top, and one on the spare wheel. We would all shout instructions at once and the car zig-zagged from one side of the road to the other, and we would shriek with laughter at the near misses. There weren't very many folk who didn't know about this incident by the time we had collected two bob from him in the safety of the grounds of Abbey House.

The first Bobby to come down through our road wearing a flat hat was called P.C. Sloper. He was very tall, but 'not too big about' though. He looked a bit on the pale-side, and his flat hat and 'short back and sides' seemed to push his ears out a little more than was necessary. He wasn't like the other Bobbies we knew. He quietly rode a big, black-framed, three-speed bicycle which moved like a whisper. It seemed as though he had no wish to stand out in a crowd, and seemed equally un-interested in finding out our names. Very strange, indeed ...

I heard Vather tell Our Mother that there was a horse by the name of Ali Sloper and he intended to do it if she would lend him the money, but she said he'd had all there was.

When we were safely out in the fields with the railings between us and P.C. Sloper, we would shout out to him as he passed by on his bike,

'Allee-ee-ee-ee-ee Slope-er-er-er-er-er!'

The first few times he took no notice and we started running for nothing. Later, he would look back at us, but continued on his way. There was something wrong here ... We had had the best of Coppers calling at our house at some time or another and this uninterested attitude just wasn't good enough!—We had our rights! And how many times was it that we had paid them a social call at the Police Station to collect Vather and wheel him home in the wooden-framed pushchair with the canvas seat? And there was the other time when we had to use

the old pram and it was so deep inside without the seats we couldn't
lift Vather out when we got home. We had to turn the lot upside down,
only to find we still couldn't remove him because he got tangled up in
the canopy and we lifted him every time we lifted the pram.

They ought to remember these things, you know—not just go cycling
past with their noses in the air!

I was walking home past the May Bush one evening . . . Right little
gentleman, I was. Our Gran was walking on the inside clutching her hand-
bag to her boney chest with both hands. I was on the outside—which is
where the men should be—so they can spit in the gutter. I was carrying
Gran's two shopping bags. One was a plain, brown leather bag with two
tasselled draw-strings around the neck and the other bag was a rather
large square one made of patchwork leather. Gran's groceries were in
the patchwork bag and her bottles were in the brown one. He had always
been a 'boddle bag', in fact, he had been a 'boddle bag' for so long that
the hard rims of the bottles were beginning to see light in a couple of
places.

I was thinking of what I should do with the penny Gran would give
me, and all of a sudden—WHOPP!

Someone had fetched me one around the ear-hole! It had come with
so much force, stealth, and surprise it had almost draped me over the
railings! I regained my balance without dropping the groceries or the
bottles in the true family tradition and, as I glanced around my throb-
bing ear, I saw a Bobby in a flat hat riding away on his bike. He turned
and gave me a broad grin.

'That's from Alley!' he shouted. I had to admire him.

Gran rushed in to examine her bottles (another family tradition), and
then asked me if I was alright. Of course I was . . . What was another
thump in the ear in a land of so many?

'I'll see thy mother about he—thee see if I don't!' she fumed. And no
wonder neither. After all, I *could* have dropped those bottles, couldn't I?

Shrewd old devil she was . . . Did you see how she decided to tell Our
Mother and not Vather? She knew Alley could beat Vather with one
hand and both feet tied in a sack. She knew who the champion was in
our house—and Gran loved to see a fair fight.

'No, don't thee do that, Gran,' I said.—'It don't matter.'

Our Mother always said, 'You only get what you deserve, and a bit
more than you ask for, sometimes.'

Well, I had just *got* something, hadn't I? I didn't fancy *asking* for a little
more from Our Mother. No . . . That would have been 'being greedy',
wouldn't it?

Acky Dock

'Where be goin' to?'

'Acky Dock. Comin'?'

'No. Got to go up town for some shoppin'.'

So the dog and I went on our own.

Acky Dock . . . Before my time, the place was called Acky Duck. They are our variations of the word 'Aquaduct', and there used to be one of these down there in the days when the canal was busy in the early 1800s.

Acky Dock is a name that now covers an area. The Cut, the Brue, the cross-line-gates, the rubbish dump, the fields, the roads, the sewer farm, Cradle Bridge . . . Each one bears the name of Acky Dock.

Acky Dock is at the end of a long, thin, grass-verged road which runs out into the moor from the railway junction. (Station Lamp will direct you.) At the end of the road is Cradle Bridge, which carries you over the River Brue to form a 'T' junction with another thin, winding road which follows the course of the River Brue. On the other side of that road is the rubbish dump and the Acky Dock sewerage works and, from there on, more and more flat fields.

It was a good place to play. Your dog troubled no one and there were no grow'd-ups to keep on to you. How to get there today? I could go down the road to Station Lamp and then out on the Moor Road. No, I'd take the short cut this time. When I say 'short cut', I don't mean it was a shorter distance. Well, it would be shorter, but it always took longer because there was always so much to do on the way.

Just before you get to Middle Lamp there are two thin metal pipes across the Cut. Someone wrapped them in sacks and covered them with pitch to keep the cold out (and it works). This sacking was attached to the pipes by wrapping barbed-wire around and round the pipes. There was just enough space between each turn of the wire to place your hands, so we would cross these with our hands on one pipe and our feet on the other looking like humpty-backed crabs out of water. If you had a dog with you (and who didn't?), he could go through the river. This crossing was not dangerous—falling-off was, but who would want to do that?

On the other side of the Cut was about six flat fields to Acky Dock.
If the grass was long you went around it to please Varmer. Never walk
across a plough ground. Climb over the gates. If you don't open them,
they don't need closing. If you find an open gate, close it—because you
you'd get blamed for it, anyroad. It doesn't matter if you can't see a
beast for miles. Close it! And don't feel offended when the farmhand
comes along and swears at you for closing the gate he had left open on
purpose to allow his horse and cart to pass through on his return trip.
He shouldn't have done it, anyroad, we would inform him with authority
from a safe distance.

Inside the plough ground was an old type of horse-drawn bus-waggon.
It was like an ordinary bus inside, and there were roundy-steps-up at
the back to go and sit up-top. There were no wheels or shafts on this
one. It had been placed there as shelter for the farmhands. 'Old Chariot'
we used to call her. We would pull the rushes from the rhines like sticks
of rhubarb and they would fly as true as any flighted arrow. The cowboys would ride in the Old Chariot and fire bullets from their paired-up
fingers . . . Kerr! Kerr! . . . and a lot of rush-armed Red Indians died
trying to get aboard that bus, I can tell you.

Another way to make the short-cut longer was when the floods were
out. Field after field would be covered with one sheet of water and you
could walk about in wellingtons in most of the places. We could tell
where the rhines and the drains were by the types of growths of withies,
rushes and reeds. ('If you can't see nothin' at all—you'm in-river!')

The seagulls would come in for a visit. Noisy devils, they are. The
other birds don't like them very much.

Have you ever played 'Hen, Pen, Duck'?—I'll bet you have! You take
a piece of slate or flat stone and you skim it over the water. As it bounces
over the surface you shout, 'Hen . . . Pen . . . Duck . . . Hen . . . ' until it
sinks. I knew a bloke who could do 'Hen, Pen, Duck' three times with
a good bit of slate.

When the floods froze over, then there was some real fun, me lads!
There was one time when we couldn't slide on it very well, though, and
this was when the ripples had been frozen into the ice. Compare this to
Niagara Falls in a frozen state and we would probably come off second
best. But have you ever seen children try to skate on a surface almost as
bad as the frozen Niagara Falls with beef rib bones tied to their feet with
string? No? . . . It's a dying art down this way, too. It was impossible . . .
and painful.

Only the posh folk from up town would have skates and this was the only time of the year when they would condescend to come and play near us. They also brought their own hockey sticks—real ones. One of them even went so far as to bring a real ice hockey stick!

We sized them up with our hobnailed boots and curved withy sticks and, armed thus, there wasn't a side that could stand against us in the rip-roaring, swiping, charging, bloody skirmish that followed called Ice Hockey. I remember a certain draper who had to return home with his skate-boot on. His foot was so swollen he couldn't get it off. Pity really, because he was almost the first bloke we had on our side with a pair of skates—but the others changed his mind.

'Have you ever played ice hockey before?' enquired the man with the ice hockey stick.

"Course I have,' replied Herby, who preferred title of 'ring leader' to 'captain'. 'And our side have won every time, s'no!'

. . . and the man *had* to believe him.

Let's get on to Acky Dock, shall we?

We arrive at Cradle Bridge. It is one of those hump-backed ones. We seldom went across it because there is huge hump-backed pipe beside it and we used to use this. It appears from one high bank and disappears into the other. If you fell from this pipe it was a long drop to the water. In summer time, you could fall a lot further, and in a dry season you might miss the water altogether. I notice of late that fanned, spike railings have been placed at each end of the pipe to make the game harder, and I'm sure the kids appreciate it.

There was fishing to do—and we used to throw stones at their floats. A better way was to make a pea-shooter out of a piece of cow parsley and shoot haws at the fishermen.

We sometimes used eel lines, but preferred the faster 'rab-all' method. You take two long withy poles and place the end of one of them through the two handles of a tin bath. You then get a piece of stiff fencing wire, put a loop in one end and fix this to another pole. Take a handful of worms and thread them on some strong cotton, and then tie this bundle of worms to the wire loop. Push the bath out onto the water. Put the bundle of worms on the river bed. Along comes an eel who takes a bite and you feel the tug on the pole. Lift the end of the pole a bit-sharpish over the bath and, if you are lucky, the eel falls into the bath. It's much quicker than fishing for them.

Then comes the rubbish dump and the sewerage works. They were side by side and surrounded with a green galvanized-tin fence with pointed tops and a sign which read 'Trespassers will be prosecuted', so we would go around the side and enter by the five-barred gate. There were lots of good things to find in there. I've known Buggle to make a bike out of the pieces he has found in there and they are not hard to find because the workmen sort them out for you and put them in a shed. They locked the shed, of course, but that presented no problem to Buggle who seemed to know how padlocks worked without using the keys. He could make most things out of something, and his mother complained he was always making something out of nothing. How do I know that?—He, and his mother could shout, and I mean shout! She was out by her front gate shouting at him once, and he was in the copse on the top of Weary All shouting back at her—and I don't think they had to repeat themselves during the course of the conversation.

The rubbish dump was also the place where we caught most of our rats. There were hundreds of them in there. We would collect food scraps and place them in an open space, and then retire out of sight. The rats would come from their tins and holes to squabble and fight for it, whilst we sat with our hand on our dog, restraining them with nothing more than a touch. How they would tremble . . . No whining . . . No barking . . . At a given signal we would lift our hands and in they would go!

Should you ever go ratting in this way—don't follow the dogs too closely. They get absorbed in their work. They get excited in their attempts to kill as many rats as possible and more often than not will bite and snap at anything that moves . . . I *know*, and you can't blame the dog for doing what he has been taught to do, can you? Get to know the other dogs, too. They all have different characters and have their likes and dislikes of certain other dogs. Two first-class ratters can prove useless if they dislike each other. They kill different ways. A terrier will snap and shake. A greyhound just snaps like the crack of a whip (and it has one of the most painful types of bite). A lurcher can favour either one of these methods, or both.

The concrete sewer tanks separated the rubbish dump from the flat, open sewer pits. These tanks were about twelve feet deep, but there was only about three feet of them showing above the ground level. Each tank had a sort of winding-wheel at each end to facilitate the filling and emptying of the tanks. When full, I wouldn't like to tell you what floated on the top in great thick layers.

It was in the middle of winter and the tanks were full. I had taken Our Young'un (Two down from me) with me and we and the dog were the only ones there. I had brought him down on the bar of one of Buggle's bikes which he had lent to me for the price of two tattered American comics.

Our Young'un wore football boots because he had a hole in his others.

I was baiting a patch when I heard those football boots clatter on the side of one of the sewer tanks. I turned quickly, just in time to see him with his foot in mid-air . . .

'Hey, whoah!—You can't walk on . . . !'

. . . and he was gone!

I went to the side of the tank and waited . . . Not a ripple! I tore off my coat, jersey and shirt and plunged my arms down through the thick, slimey layer . . . God, it was cold! I couldn't find him . . . I'd have to go down deeper . . . and my chin started to submerge . . . (Don't make a wave? There was no fear of that. It was too solid!) I took no notice of the smell because I was so worried . . . No, I didn't smell it, but I could taste it for days afterwards though!

I frantically fished about with my arms . . . I couldn't breathe through my runny nose . . . I breathed through my mouth with short, sharp, goldfish-like puffs . . . and then my hand touched something a little more solid than the rest so I grabbed-hold and yanked upwards! Up came Our Young'un with a piece of soggy newspaper stuck inside his collar. He let out a bawl that could have been heard on the other side of Tor Hill and started to gasp and gulp.

I suspected he had been holding his breath because he would never have been able to shout like that, otherwise. I stood him up . . . He hollered 'he couldn't open his eyes' and bellered 'he were cold'. I felt so sorry for him, but could no more cuddle or comfort him that I could pick my own nose at that moment. I had to do something with him though—so I took him across the road and chucked him in-river! I washed my face, chest and arms. That water was freezing-cold! Our Young'un started making for the bank, but I wouldn't let him land.

'Thee get down underneath first!' I told him.

'I can't!—I be cood!'

I shoved him underneath . . . It was cruel, I know . . .

'Sorry, Young'un,' I said, 'but you ain't goin' home stinking like that on the bar of that bike—not with I peddlin' it, anyroad!'

I got him home as quickly as possible. We must have got used to the smell, too, because as soon as we got through the front door Our Mother exclaimed, 'Cooh!—Where have 'ee been with thy smeech?'

'He were pickin' some forget-me-nots, Mother, and falled in-ditch.'

'What?—This time of year?'

'Well, they looked like forget-me-nots!'

We got found out in the end. A bloke up-Pub told Vather. He had seen me chuck the Little'un in-river. Well, what could I do then? I had to tell the truth then, didn't I?

And do you know what?

The truth *does* hurt, sometimes . . .

Bald-headed men working with chicken dung have re-grown their hair again. I now have a bald head—but I have a beard. Do you think . . . ?

Well, try it, if you wish. Personally, I don't think I mind being bald-headed.

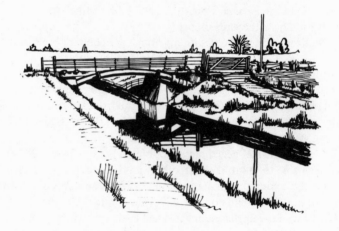

What's up Out-in-Moor

That long, thin, dusty line to Acky Dock . . . Each side of the road were grass verges. Each side of the verges were the rhines with a liberal scattering of withies and bramble bushes.

We were walking out into the moor in the early evening when we saw the front wheel of a bicycle sticking up out of the grass beside the rhine. 'What's up?' we wondered . . . Had there been an accident? . . . Had someone fallen from his bike?

Beside the bike we found Dustbin Douglas sleeping it off. Almost an expected situation, really, because it was Market Day and 'they' were open all day. Dustbin Douglas was not one of the 'dustbin' blokes. To go to and from the town he had to pass rubbish dump—hance the nickname. Dirty Fred was the dustman. He wasn't a dirty bloke, but his lot was a dusty one because fifty per cent of the refuse was clinkers and ashes. Most of the fine ash was sifted out and resold for the manufacture of mortar.

Dustbin Douglas had been there quite some time. It hadn't rained since early in the afternoon and his clothes was damp.

'Come on, Doug, wake up!'

He stirred . . . 'I'm alright,' he muttered. (Was there ever a drunk who wasn't?)

'Wake up, Doug. You'm soaked through and you'll catch thy death a cold!'

He stirred again . . . 'I'm alright—I be alright!' . . . He took in his surroundings. 'What be you-lot doin' here?'

'Tryin' to wake thee up. You'm soaked right through!'

He checked this information . . . 'Looksee, so I be . . . What time is it? . . . Half-past five?! . . . Is it now? . . . Better be gettin' on home, I spose . . .'

Could he manage? . . . Yes, he could manage, and thanks for 'looking out' to him.

At about the same time on another Market Day I saw a stationary pony and float on the road. One of the wheels were broken. Hullo? What's

up? . . . Had there been an accident? And where else would one leave a
pony and float with a broken wheel, you may ask?

Everything looked wrong from the start, you see. A normal bloke
would unharness the pony and ride it away for help. He could also unharness the horse and tie it to a gate or something. And he wouldn't
leave the cart blocking the narrow road. Something *was* up!

Mokus, the driver, was asleep in the bottom of the float snoring his
head off with one and a half flagons of cider cuddled-up in his arms. I
shook him . . . 'I'll bet he's alright,' I thought to myself.

'Hey, Mokus! You've busted a wheel!'

'I've what?!' . . . Yes, he was 'alright', alright.

The metal rim had come off and the rotten old wheel had broken. He
moodily looked at the unrepairable damage. We moved the float off the
road, and he unharnessed the pony.

Did I know Mr Redman? Mr Redman was the local wheelright-come-
blacksmith. Yes, I knew him alright.

Would I go and tell him what was up?—He'd give a penny for going,
but he didn't have much change on him at the moment. This, roughly
translated, meant there was no point in paying a child to do something
he may not do. That was fair enough, so I accepted.

. . . and would I come back and tell him if everything was alright? For
a penny?

Well . . . It was all he could afford . . . He wasn't made of money and
that wheel was going to cost him a tidy bit . . .

'Alright?' he asked, and offered his over-peat-worked hand.

We spit and shook hands . . . It made me feel proud.

Mr Redman laughed and said he expected as much. He said he would
see to it right away and not to bother to return to Mokus, so I went
home.

Three days later, Our Mother told me, 'There's somethin' on the table
for thee. A man left it, and he said "Thank the Young'un very much".'
There, on the table, surrounded by thousands of silent, smiling, friendly
brothers, was a paper bag—a bag of Golden Charms toffees. It wasn't the
pointed kind of sweet packet—it was one of the bigger, square kind. It
looked as though it had been in a busy pocket for some time because it
was worn through in places and some of the toffees protruded through.
Beside the paper bag was a penny . . . It had Queen Victoria's head on it.

What was there about Mokus that made me feel so different? He would
sometimes pass me in his float with two new wheels and he would then
nod in my direction and raise his whip. I, in return, would raise my hand

(just like the grow'd ups did), and neither one of us ever needed to say 'thank you'.

I was walking back from Rubbish Dump with the dog. Rat tails were a penny for five at the Council Yard.

We had had a long spell of rain and the two nearest fields to Cradle Bridge weren't flooded, but they were a little more than soggy. It was very misty. It was getting dark, and I decided to walk along the road 'a whiles' before crossing the fields to home. Strange how the mist seemed to blanket the sounds, almost the same as a 'falling' of snow.

We arrived at the emmet heap and the two large tufts of marsh reed on the verge, and we were just about to cross the rhine into the fields when the dog growled, short and low. Our dog didn't growl for no reason. We stopped and remained silent. What was up? I placed my hand on the Airedale's neck. An Airedale's coat is always stiff and bristly . . . It bristled-stiffer now!

'Is anyone there?' a voice called from the mist.

He didn't sound like anyone I knew.

'Is anyone there, please?' he shouted again.

He definitely sounded like a 'foreigner'. I asked him what was up.

'I am frightfully sorry to bother you, but I appear to be lost. Would you help me, please?'

Lost—on *this* road? He *must* be a foreigner!

Another five yards of cautious approach and I could see him stood by the gate on the other side of the road. He was oldish—hiking jacket, plus-fours, zig-zag-knitted pullover and stockings—and, with that deerstalker hat, he *had* to be a stranger!

Where had he come from?—UP TOWN?!

'Yes, I am staying with friends and decided to take a short walk. The mist seemed to thicken rather quickly.'

Yes, it *was* thick, and it *had* come-down a bit-fast.

Had I just come from the town? (No wonder he got lost!)

No, I hadn't. Town was t'other way.

Yes, I would take him back.

No, it wasn't no bother. It wasn't much out of the way.

No, I couldn't see any further than he could.

No, I never got lost. I didn't know how-to.

No, I hadn't never been to Burtle Moor. Eight miles was too far away.

Yes, the dog would help me if I did get lost. (I suppose so, anyroad.)

The questions that man asked!

We arrived at Station Lamp. No, no good. Would I assist him further?
We arrived at Saint Benedict's church without meeting anyone. Well, he
wasn't quite sure. I delivered him to the George and Pilgrim. (His friends
lived in the right place, anyroad.)

'Thank you very much, Young Man. I am very deeply indebted to
you. Here is a little something for the trouble I have caused you.')

I took the proffered coin with my empty left hand and thanked him.
A florin!—Two bob! I thanked him again, sir. He smiled and offered me
his right hand to wish me goodbye. I transferred the bundle of rat tails
to my left hand . . . wiped my hand on the thigh of my trousers, and
shook his hand. We didn't spit because that isn't allowed in the George
and Pilgrim. A very nice bloke—for a 'foreigner'. I was glad he had friends.
All those questions he had asked me . . . I had learnt something from
them. If you walk a straight line in the dark and you falter—you're lost!

The Moor wasn't just there for the floods, ratting and farming, you
know. Further afield was Turf Moor, which name covers any part of
the moor where the peat was cut in 'turfs'—where Mrs Jones came from,
remember? Certain parts of Turf Moor were known as Common Land
where certain folk could go and cut the peat they needed. Old Bert,
who lived next door, would have been eighty-four this year. He used to
recall when he helped his father to do this.

Turf Moor floats on brackish water like a blanket of thick peat. If a
herd of cows ran past you, you could feel the ground undulate beneath
your feet in long slow waves. The peat was cut in long narrow pits about
six to eight feet wide. The peat workers would cut out a spit, spade-
square and spade-deep. This spit was called a 'mump'. The 'mump' was
split into three biscuit-like 'turfs' and two of these would be placed
leaning one against the other with the other one on the top to dry out a
little. When they were ready, they were placed round and like loose bricks
in piles as high as a man or woman could reach. These were called
'ruckles' and this completed the drying operation.

Digging the first and second layers could be hard work and it got far
more difficult as the depth progressed. The depth would be decided by
the 'mabby', which is the bottom layer. If this was broken, the digger
goes down through into the water. If the 'diggin'' is left for about twenty
years, the water will bring more peat from underneath and refill the hole.

Yes . . . out-in-moor could be a wonder and a mystery—even to those
who knew her.

Just before Dumpsy

I had a small job—selling meat pies in the pubs on Friday and Saturday nights. I would comb my hair to do this; after all, I had to look 'a bit smiggit', didn't I?

'Comb it', did I say? Short back, sides, and top, were the orders of the day in our house. Mine was so short it was impossible to put a parting in it regardless of the amount of 'Adam's Oil' I poured on from the water tap. Still, if there wasn't enough to comb there wasn't enough to catch hold of, and that was very important.

I had to leave home early in the evening whilst the other young'uns were playing in the road. How I hated passing some of them, knowing that they could see I had attempted to comb my hair.

> Bluebells, cockle shells.
> Easy . . . I see . . . Ov-err . . .

Cooh. Didn't they-girls and the young'uns used to skip in that road? There would be a bunch of them with a rope right-across-road and they would take it in turns to jump in . . . skip a bit . . . and jump out again.

> She is lovely. She is pretty.
> She's the pride of Lundun City.
> She comes a'courtin', one, two, three.
> Please will you tell us
> Who it can be? . . .

And small groups with the small hand-skipping ropes . . .

> The big ship sails through the Illy-ally-oo.
> The Ally-ally-oo. The Ally-ally-oo . . .

Skipping . . . Skipping . . . All singing and skipping . . .
'Oh? Goin' sellin' they-pies then?'
'Ah, I be, Missiz Jack.'

'Well, you do look a bit tidier than usual, I must say. Look a lot better like that, you do. Don't ur look betterer, Missiz Juggs?'

'Ah. He do look a bit better for a change.'

> The big ship sails through the Illy-ally-oo,
> The last day of Sep-tem-ber . . .

All in our road—a road covered with hopscotch and writing—and not one foul word among the lot. 'R.B. loves S.H.'—Who wrote that? . . . The daft fools . . .

Hopscotches . . . Hopscotches of all shapes and sizes . . . Four squares with the criss-cross in the middle . . . There was one with five-brace of squares . . . The wriggly-round one with 'Home' in the middle, like a snail . . . Some had been drawn and re-drawn over and over again . . . Some were wearing away because the road was too rough, or because of the hole in the middle . . . Some had dropped into a state of disuse because the tar had seeped through . . . and some had a patch of dried horse dung.

> Mother's in the kitchen doin' a bit of stitchin'.
> In comes a black girl and chucks her OUT!

The road-games from path to path . . .

'Please Jack, can we cross the water?'

'No!'

. . . and how they did 'hurn' across the road . . . all of a scrabble . . . hoping not to be 'touched'.

'You can't touch I!—I weren't even in the water!'

'Maybe you weren't—but you had your foot in the gutter. You'm *IT!*'

(That's right, young'un. You tell him!?)

'Be goin' up town, me son?'

'Ah, I be. Can I take thy bottles up for thee?'

(Good, dear Old Regg'o . . . All we-young'uns like him so much.)

'I've got um here ready. One of the bwoys'll bring um back for me. Gie Lan'lard my regards, will 'ee?'

'Ah, I will' (anything for you, Regg'o).

> One, two, three, a'lary.
> Sarah Jane went down the dairy.
> One pint . . . two pints . . . three pints . . .

Girls playing 'ball' and bouncing them about . . . Up and down, on the path and in the road . . . against the walls. Playing there, with their dresses turned up into the elastic legs of their navy blue knickers—the same as they did when they played handstands against the hedges . . .

No marbles, no cocky-five-stones, no hoops, no tippit . . . No . . . They would have to wait until the whip-and-top season was over . . . and whip-and-top doesn't go well with hopscotch, you know . . .

'If he comes on here again, I shall chuck un, mind!'

Tops . . . Round tops . . . Tops like a 'T' all-round . . . Tops that slope to a point in a curve . . . Red tops, green tops, yeller tops . . . Tops with different coloured stripes—all with a hobnail in the bottom to keep them spinning . . . and spinning . . .

> Under the moon
> and over the stars . . .

'Missiz Wills'. (Don't think she knows me with me hair combed.)

'Missiz Wick'. (Don't answer now, me dear. Wait 'til I get down by Station.)

> Big Ben strikes, one, boom-boom, two, boom-boom.
> Three-boom, four-boom, five, boom-boom . . .

There's no end to it, you know. Cricket by Snooks's Lamp . . . Hide and seek . . .

> Big Ben strikes, six, boom-boom, seven, boom-boom.
> Eight-boom, nine-boom, ten, boom-boom . . .

. . . and there was bows and arrows . . . football . . . cowboys and injuns . . .

'Oh, don't ur look lovely with his hair combed-smiggit?'

Damn! The older blokes had sneaked up on me. I hadn't seen them.

'Ho, ho! And who's little bwoy be you, then?'

'And who were it who chucked our clothes in-river while we were swimmin', I'd like to know?'

'It weren't I, Sid!'

'T'were. I saw thee!'

'You didn't then, 'cos you were down in Big Hole when . . . !' (Oh, dear I . . .)

'Grab-hold of him, Herby . . . I'll help thee . . . Perce, thee give un a dose of the fizzick!'

'So t'were he who done it, were it?—Never did find thiick towel of mine!'

. . . And no wonder . . . He lost one of mine back-along and laughed about it. I couldn't bring myself to chuck his towel in-river. It was a thick, new one . . . and we were still using it up-home. 'I found it,' I'd told Our Mother.

The dreaded fizzick was applied. Bunched knuckles were rubbed quickly and firmly up and down the stubble on the back of my head. Oh, it hurt! They released me and laughed loudly as I tried to withdraw my head into my shoulders. It burnt even more now that the rubbing had stopped—like a touch of the spree on the back of the head!

They wouldn't have touched me if I hadn't been tidy! Never mind. They have all got bikes . . . They'll leave them unguarded one day . . . I'll kick their spokes in!

. . . And the young'uns still played in the road without stopping to watch what was going on . . . Still chanting . . . Still singing . . .

> Teddy Bear, Teddy Bear, touch the ground.
> Teddy Bear, Teddy Bear, turn around . . .

(Always stop and let the hoss and cart go through . . . Keep out of the way of the wheels . . . Don't frighten the hoss and make him shy . . .)

> Teddy Bear, Teddy Bear, climb the stairs.
> Teddy Bear, Teddy Bear, say your prayers . . .

(And don't hang-on the back of the cart when he've gone by!)

> Teddy Bear, Teddy Bear, dowt the light.
> Teddy Bear, Teddy Bear, say goodnight . . .

Nearly all gone, now . . .

Oh, motorcar, with your stronger-lighted lights . . . Looksee what you've done!

Pure Poetry

Did the poetry and verse end when I left the familiar boundaries of 'Our Road'?—Did these poems and songs cease with the happiness of childhood?

No. It went on and on . . . and on . . .

At about 7.30 p.m. I would collect my basket of pies from Florrie Brown's. Meat, onion, and potato pies, they were. Tuppence a'piece, and they were worth it. They were good! There were special times (like Tor Fair, for instance), when she would make cheese and onion pies as well. These were threepence, and they were worth it, too. This wasn't just my opinion. Florrie Brown knew her job and those pies sold like . . . hot cakes?

There were a lot of pubs and I visited most of them. There was never a time when the Landlord told me that children were not allowed on the premises. I did as instructed by Florrie . . . Go in . . . Sell my pies . . . Wish the Landlord goodnight . . . thank him . . . and depart.

There were times when this routine was interrupted.

I knew Mr Parker was a tailor. He was always well dressed. I entered the backroom of the Mitre. A small room, smokey . . . There were benches and tables around the room . . . a big fireplace . . . The settle started from beside the fireplace and came out square into the room to form a sort of passage between two doors.

A piano started to play . . . Mr Parker got up from the settle and leant against the 'clavvy-tack'—the shelf above the mantlepiece and, with his half-pint in one hand and his large pipe in the other, he commenced to sing . . .

> There's many a sailor
> asleep in the deep . . .
> So beware . . . beware . . .

What a wonderful voice . . . So deep . . . I had never heard anything so beautiful.

'Come on, me son. Don't hang about, there's a good bwoy' . . .

There was a backroom in the Globe. They were already having a sing-
song before I arrived and, as I entered, they were coaxing an old man
'just to have one go'. The voice was old and mellow . . . it was soft and
pleasant as he sang his song, and then, slowly going down onto one
knee, he sang the chorus to an old lady in the corner seat,

> Liza. Lovely Liza,
> I'll never love none but thee.
> Bide with I, me own true love,
> And ever I'll bide with thee . . .

'Got any cheese pies tonight, me son?—Why not? . . . '

> . . . . and
> We'll be happy as ducks and drakes,
> Every night and mornin' . . .

'Let's have three of they-pies, me dear, will 'ee?'
     . . . and amidst the cheers and loud applause the old man returned to
his seat beside his 'own true love' and gently took her hand . . . She
beamed so proudly . . .
     'Hey, Young'un. Be we goin' to get any of they-pies tonight?'
     Off to the First and Last where hard times and hard folk seemed to
live in harmony with a pint of cider. There was always so much noise
and laughter. Shouts of encouragement 'egged' a huge farm labourer to
another verse—with the end of each one being punctuated with noisy
gulps from a quart pot.

> One night as I did a'walk down the Strand,
> I met a fair creature who 'looked-up' so grand.
> She'd jewels and such finery as ever'd behold,
> And said she were a virgin of nineteen-year-old.

'How much be they-pies, Young'un?'
'Come on, Tomm'o. The pianner's leavin' thee behind!'
(A quick wipe of the mouth with the back of the hand . . .)

> The weddin' party broke up and we retired to rest,
> And me hair stood on end while me young bride undressed.
> A cartload of paddin', did she start to unfold,

Which I thought were b'culiar for a nineteen-year-old.

'Careful!—There's a young pie-bwoy here, mind!'
'Better hurry up, me son. This ain't for young bwoys to hear . . . '
Alright . . . Thank you everybody . . . G'night, Lan'lord . . . There
were the young and noisy topers, helping one another along the streets,
without seeming to mind who listened to them . . . They would sing
of the local lady of easy virtue . . .

> Old Titty Blue Drawers.
> Old Tatty Blue Drawers,
> With a hole in the middle
> For Titty to piddle.
> Old Titty Blue Drawers.

Before? . . . There were the tales Our Mother told to me . . . about
when she and Uncoo Awffy were 'little' and they happened to pass the
open door of the Tap on a warm summer evening.

An old man was singing. They stopped . . . They could see him stood
beside an old straight-backed piano. Upon the piano was a photograph
of the Landlady in a gilt frame and, with one arm placed loosely about
the picture and the other holding his pot on high, he sang,

> She was only a beautiful picture
> In a beautiful golden frame.

The song ended with the most thunderous, most worthy applause they
had ever heard. They were enthralled. The old man saw them through
the open door and came out to them. They shouldn't be there, he told
them . . . They ought to be home in bed, Gramf said.

I entered the King Bill . . . Vather didn't usually come in there, yet
here he was on this occasion. He was giving them a rendering of one of
his Dobbin-type songs without the accompaniment of the piano, because
there was no set tune to follow when Vather sung.

> 'Oh, mother, can I go out to play?'
> 'Yes, my darlin' daughter,
> But mind the fishes don't bite thy neck,
> So keep in under the water' . . .

The crowd joined in with an uninvited chorus . . .

> Shut thy mouth. Do shut thy mouth.
> Oh, do thee shut thy mouth.
> Oh, shut thy mouth, Do shut thy mouth.
> Oh, do thee shut thy mouth.

Encouraged thus, Vather continued . . .

> T'were Chris'miss Day in the Workhouse.
> The whitewashed walls were black.
> A bwoy, bare-footed with his boots on,
> Stood-seated on his back.
>
> Why do 'ee sit there-standin'
> With jamjars stuck on thy head?
> Go home and swim with a bucket or a tin,
> But don't thee get out of bed . . .

The pianist stirred the crowd to another chorus . . .

> Sit down you sod. Sit down you sod.
> Sit down you sod, sit down.
> Sit down you sod. Sit down you sod.
> Oh, do sit down you sod, sit down.

Vather beamed at this accolade of abuse. Marvellous! He'd got them one hundred per cent against him. The smile fell from his face as his eyes alighted on me.

'Hoy, thee!' he bellowed. 'OUT!'

'Hey, Swiggy,' said the Landlord, 'I'll do the chuckin' out in here!'

'Here, here!' murmured the crowd.

I smiled leeringly at Vather.

'And take that look off of thy face!' he hollered at me. 'You'm evil, you be! Bloody evil!'

'Shame. Shame! Poor little'un,' the crowd chanted.

I held my pie basket to my chest and bowed in mock acceptance to Vather.

Cooh!—Didn't that crowd applaud my exit?

Earning a Living

As we got older, most of us took jobs up town, and we did these jobs after school and on Saturdays. I said *'most'* of us. The farmer's sons had been working a seven-day week from the time they had learned to walk, and we others could guess what type of beasts there were on a particular farm by the smell of the son's clothing.

Now, please—I don't mean they smelled dirty. There was the acrid smell of horse sweat, the sweet smell of cows, the damp, woolly smell of sheep, and the smell of pigs. Like me, they had only the one pair of boots, and those classrooms could be rather warm at times.

There were the sons of shopkeepers. They didn't get themselves jobs and they didn't help their fathers—that was *our* jobs. No, they had to get on with their homework and get on in the world. These errand-boy jobs averaged out at about eighteen hours a week or more, and average wage was half-a-crown a week. This was not pocket money. It was handed over to Our Mother to 'help-keep', and she would give three-pence back. The school inspector didn't approve of these jobs and every time the complaints arrived at school I would leave my job, as instructed, and find another somewhere else. There were a whole bunch of us moving around like counters on a draught-board.

I ran errands for two butchers. The first one sent me to the slaughter-house and they killed a cow whilst I was there. A sow with a broken leg was brought in by horse and float, and I still hear its screams to this day. I couldn't go to school for two days afterwards, and no one needed to tell me to get another job.

The other butcher and his wife were a very nice old couple. It was a pleasure to work for them and they gave me a pound of sausages with my wages every week. For one certain customer the butcher would place a bone upon the family joint. There were usually two or three tradesmen awaiting my arrival at the front gate of the house. There was a bull terrier in there and no one entered until she had had her bone. Made me feel like a king, it did.

I did a couple of grocery rounds. Both of them entailed the riding of those shop-bikes with the carrier and a small wheel in the front. Neither one of them would think anything of sending me three or four miles overloaded with cardboard boxes of groceries.

On one of these trips I delivered the last order to a lady's house out in the country. The day was hot and I was thirsty, so I asked her for a drink of water. 'Does your mother know that you do go round beggin'?' she asked me. I didn't take that glass of water, but I said 'thank you', just the same. The next time I arrived at her place she opened the door to allow me to carry the heavy box of groceries into her kitchen and place them on the table. My eyes lit up as I saw the newly baked cake cooling on the wire mat on the table. The lady moved in quickly—but too late. I smashed it to a pulp with the box of groceries. I apologised, but she told the grocer just the same. I heard her reporting to him . . . 'He said he were sorry, but he had thiick sort of a look in his eye' . . . She was right, I hadn't grinned or laughed, but I wanted her to see 'thiick look'.

Like all businesses, we had our troubles. The second grocer was a right old skinflint and stuck to his money like ticks to a dog's back. He would break out into a sweat at the thought of handing some change to a customer. I used to love to see him trying to smile and be friendly to someone who had not spent enough in his shop.

There were some rotten bastards about! Before my errand days Our Mother had to pay two week's rent out of the dole money because the collector couldn't come around for the rent on the following Christmas week. This meant sixteen shillings and sixpence had to be taken from the eighteen shillings and sixpence dole money, and I don't think he wished us a happy Christmas.

Mother sent me up to the grocer to ask if she could cancel the half-crown Christmas cake on order. 'No, she couldn't do that,' he said, 'because so many other people were doing it.'

'God rest that merry gentleman,' and the sooner the better!

Mr Sweet, the insurance man, managed to get ten shillings for us from the British Legion, because Gramf and Vather had been in the army, so we had a happy Xmas.

Old Skinflint and the Merry Gentleman were one and the same person. He had forgotten about the incident, but I hadn't and, when he paid me the usual two-and-six for working a forty-four hour week whilst on holiday, I decided he had had a long enough run.

'What's this?' I asked him.

'Half-a-crown a week, I pay thee,' he said, 'and half-a-crown you've got!'

Most of the time Our Mother bought cheese when Vather told her to get some more. I kept that cheese dish stocked and Vather didn't have to ask for several months. Uncoo Awby and Uncoo Bob received cheap crushed Woodbines. I crushed the packets myself. They wouldn't have taken good fags from me at a cheap rate! Our young'uns began to get fussy about the type of chocolate biscuits they would like next.

I grabbed what was going at every opportunity. It went on and on and on, and I didn't care or worry in the slightest because I felt I was getting my own back, but there came the day when I suddenly realized that the opportunities were not only becoming more often but were more easily available.

What was it Old Regg'o had told me? 'We can catch birds and rabbits 'cos they do keep on doin' the same things the same way. Now, Varmer and the Game Keeper do know this as well, so 'tis up to thee to do the same things you shouldn't be doin'—diff'rent!—Don't make patterns, see?'

I know this advice was given to me for my minor ventures into poaching, which isn't really stealing, but I suddenly realized that I didn't like the feeling of being 'poached'.

I pondered on my situation. I wouldn't be going on the rounds for the next couple of hours because I had to clean the brass weights and scales. I was the only one in the shop at that moment, so I couldn't go outside without asking. I returned today's packet of Woodbines to the shelf and, when the grocer returned to his post from his extra long cup of tea, I gave in my notice.

One of the happiest jobs I ever had was working on a milk round. It was harder work—seven days a week, and twice a day in the summer because the milk wouldn't keep.

Five bob a week they paid me, plus some of my meals because the job started rather early in the morning. There was breakfast after doing part of the round, then off to school with my lunch for 'nunch-time'. There was also tea and supper in the summertime . . . All good farm food.

And I could eat! 'Cheaper to keep thee for a week than a fortnight,' Missiz would say with a laugh. She liked to feel her cookery was appreciated and I could dispose of a meal with one hundred per cent flattery without uttering a word. Old Ernie, the milk roundsman, would jokingly shout, 'Hurry up and give un some bread and cheese to finish up with, Clara!—And whip the tablecloth off while he's busy in case he makes a sangwich out of that as well.'

I never made any retorts. You can't talk and eat properly at the same time. You might choke!

They put the finishing touches to my table manners. They weren't snobbish about it. They were glad to have me and I was glad to be with them. They treated me like a *bloke*. They showed me how to do things and explained *why* they were done that way. They gave me *my own* money bag, *my own* smock, *my own* milk can with *my own* pint and half-pint measures hanging inside of it.

We sold some of the milk in bottles—the type with the press-in milk tops made of cardboard—but most of it was sold from the can and measured into the customers' jugs . . . with a drop-extra to make up for what may have been spilt during the pouring operation.

Ah, yes, I want you to listen to this, now. Some of the customers would ask, 'Can I have a pint of one-cow's milk for the Babb, please?'— And they would get it! Try asking your present-day milkman for that and see how you get on!

We did the milkround by horse and float (with the gert shiny churn up-front). The horse was called Tom and knew the round better than we did. I liked Tom, but he hated everyone except Ernie, and tried to bite me every time I went close to his head.

Ernie once accepted too many Christmas boxes and I had to finish off the round with him lying in the bottom of the float. Tom made his own way home, but I had my full share of power just holding the unanswered reins. It was marvellous to feel so important. We reached the yard without incident and Ernie was handed over to the tender mercies of the womenfolk. This left me with Ernie's job, which was far more important than the washing of milk churns and cans, and removing the cream marks from the insides of the bottles with a hand brush.

I unloaded the bottles and cans. Dismantled the gert big churn from its strapped position and paused . . . Ernie was still washed-out, so I decided to go ahead and bed the horse down. I un-hixxed the harness from the float . . . supported the weight of the shafts . . . and told Tom to 'giddup'. He walked two or four paces clear of the shafts and stopped. (He'd done this before, and wasn't going to be told to 'whoah' with every Tom, Dick, or Harry that happened along.) I lowered the shafts to the ground, and then went to take hold of his bridle. He tried to bite me! I stood in front of him—out of range of those teeth.

'Now looksee here, Tom!' I said. 'Any more of that and you can bide out here 'til tomorrow. And with all thy harness on!'

Tom stared at me . . . I stared at him . . . (and I think he won, mind,

but I didn't let on). I took hold of the bridle again . . . led him into the
stable . . . unharnessed him . . . rubbed him down whilst he got stuck
into his feed . . . and spread the bedding. No trouble at all! He was
already in the shafts when I arrived next morning. I had brought him an
apple for Christmas . . . I walked quietly to his head, and he tried to
bite me.

Ernie was back 'in harness' . . . I wasn't needed any more.

On a certain part of the round we had to come down a very steep hill.
It was a bad hill when the weather was fine, but we had even rougher
times in the winter. True, we would have frost nails put in Tom's shoes
and they were a big help, but there were times when things became 'a
bit much'—like the time when Ernie and I were walking Tom down hill
on a frosty morning, and Ernie had taken the horse's head. The road
suddenly went like black glass and down went Tom with Ernie beneath
him!

I slammed on the brake-tight. Jambed the chain-block under the
wheel. Grabbed a big stone from someone's nearby wall and placed it
under the other wheel. I then took the three sack bags from the float
and spread them close to Tom's head . . . No, not enough! So I took off
my smock and jacket and spread them as well. I stepped close to Tom's
head . . . took a firm hold on both sides of his bridle . . . pressed my
face close to his . . . and slowly pushed his head upwards and backwards.
Up he came . . . slowly . . . and poor old Ernie let out such a bellow!
'Ohhhh!—Go on. Go on!'

Tom had one of his frost-studded feet on Ernie's thigh!

And 'go on', I did. We couldn't do the round without Tom, you see?

Tom stood firmly with his forefeet on the sacks. Ernie scrabbled
about on hands and knees to spread my smock and jacket beneath the
hindlegs . . . He examined Tom's knees and his haunches . . . Checked
the shafts . . . the churn straps . . .

'Cooh, that's lucky,' he said. 'No damage at all, but my leg don't half
give I "gipper", though!'

'Can 'ee manage, Ernie?' I enquired.

'Ah, I 'spect I can muggo along . . . Thee do the long uns and I'll do
the shart uns . . . '

He busied himself with my anti-slide-precautions and then looked at
me and laughed.

'I thought you two weren't friends,' he said. 'You can keep-hold the
head for the rest of the way down, if you like. It don't look too bad
from here, s'no.'

I then realized I was still close to Tom's head. Those horses know, you know.

We got our milk from a farm. Nice old place, it was. Varmer and Missiz were a nice couple, too. They always called me 'young man'.

As I got a little more competent on the milkround I found myself with time to spare, so it naturally followed that I should spend this time 'doin' fillin'-in jobs' at the farm. Nothing steady—just things like haymaking, harvesting, mangle and chaff grinding, pig and calf feeding, cleaning harness, tack, and implements, mucking-out and dung-humping, etc. . . There were all the technical names to learn:

Muck-out: Clean up the stall or stable and move it outside.
Dung-up: Load the putt.
Dung-hump: Take it to where it is required.
Muck-spread: Chuck it about—evenly—with a dung fork, not a pick.

Someone once mentioned 'dung walloping'—to beat the dried cow-pancakes about out in the fields. I was also informed (with tongue in cheek) that this was also called 'Ka-Ka-thumpin''. 'The lyin' toads!' I thought. 'They'm talkin' about 'turd-bashin'!

A stranger must always beware when walking behind cows in a cow stall. Strangers make them nervous and they kick backwards with great accuracy. I was warned of this and gave the cows the respect they deserved.

I was about to pass behind one, once, and she raised her tail and commenced to answer a call to nature which had gone in at the other end as spring grass. It poured out in a semi-liquid stream landing in the channel-drain behind her, and, keeping close to the wall, which was about five feet from the danger point, I attempted to pass in safety. The cow coughed and the boiling hot dung hit me fair and square, covering me from the top of my head down to my waist! Semi-liquid, it might be, but it is impossible to see through it—at that temperature, anyroad!

Six huge, farm-worked hands, each holding a bundle of straw dipped in a bucket of cold water, silently rubbed me down with a gentleness that could have made a stiff brush obsolete, and I could feel them trembling. As I opened my eyes they shrieked with laughter to the man. They were experts at 'muck-spreading' and they had made a first class job of me!

I liked haymaking . . . There was a time when it was all done by hand—with scythes, hand-rakes, and picks. The old hands used to tell me. Everything was up to date when I started though. The only parts to be scythed

were around the sides of the field and in the close vicinity of the odd
tree in the field. Then the horse would come in pulling the mower
behind him . . . A wonderful thing to watch . . .

When the sun had 'had a bit of a go' at one side of the mown grass,
we would turn it over with picks. Later, the horse-rake would drag the
hay into 'rollers', long lines of hay across the field, and then the rollers
would be separated into 'pooks' in preparation for the loading of the
horse-drawn haywain.

The haywain would travel between two lines of pooks, and we would
load it—two or three on the ground and one up-top the load, or three or
four on the ground and two up-topsides. 'Let the pick (or 'peek') do the
work,' that's what they used to tell me. It didn't make sense at first,
but I soon got the idea because it's a lot easier that way.

A good horse doesn't need someone by his head. He would do as he
was told. Nice, pleasant, shouting, it was, and usually by the same person
each time to avoid confusing the horse. (Too many cooks?) Should there
be a plague of the inevitable 'can I help' young'uns, there was always a
rush and squabble to take up the position at the horse's head. Once
selected, he would then be given the quickest apprenticeship in existence.

'Wait for I to tell thee, and mind you keep out of the way of the hoss's
feet!'

'Up-top!'—That's to inform the men on the load that the waggon is
about to move, and they would rest the prongs of their picks in the load
to steady themselves.

'Giddup . . . heyyyyy-uh . . . heyyyy-uh . . . ' A nice steady start was
needed.

'Giddup!'—Move—Hurry up . . . There's a difference, you see?

Now . . . When the horse is on the road the carter would walk on the
path-side of him and would shout 'Cum-yer' to bring the horse closer
to the path. A little too much and the wheels would 'ground' against
the kerb, so the carter would shout 'Wug-aaf', and the horse would move
a little further out into the road. Out-in-field, you may find yourself
shouting instructions to the horse from the other side of him. Should
this be so, you would shout 'Wug-aaf' to tell the horse to come towards
you—to *his* right. To move him away from you—to *his* left, you would
have to shout 'Cum-yer'.

This used to 'muggo' me up a little at first, but I can honestly say I
have never known any of the horses to find any difficulty with the
arrangement.

'Who-o-o-ah'—Steady now . . . stop. A nice and easy sort of shout. 'Whoah!'—Stop!—Behave!

There was a sound, a sort of encouraging sort of sound to get the horse to pull better. You drag air into the mouth with the tongue pressed tightly against one side of the roof of the mouth. It sounds like,

'Gdddttt . . . Gdddttt . . . Come on, Samson . . . Giddup, son.' Son?— Most of them were big enough to make a dozen Gramfers! But they were gentle, so gentle—more 'gentler' than twenty loving old Grans.

I liked harvesting as well. Ernie and I usually had to go to other farms to do this. Ernie would be hired by the farmer, and I would go along as 'exter'. They had a horse-drawn reaping machine which cut the 'carn' *and tied it into sheaves!*—That's progress for you. The odd sheaf or two would come undone and we would then re-tie it with twisted-straws, just like they did in the old days when the corn had been cut with reap-hooks. (The others told me that.)

My job would be stacking the sheaves in 'stooks' . . . Some folk call a 'stook' a 'stitch'. Depends on where you come from, I suppose. You grab two sheaves under your arms and ram the bottoms onto the ground with the heads together and the bottoms kicked out a bit . . . Stack another two in the same way beside them . . . Two more, and these lean in on the other four . . . Two more at the other end in the same way and this stops them from falling over.

Fresh air . . . Sun on your back . . . Birds singing . . . Sounds like a nice job, doesn't it?—You should try following it for a day though.

Those ears of corn would cut and scratch the insides of my arms and it was like having a 'touch of the blood-raw spree'. I tried covering my arms with a pair of old stockings with the feet cut off. Varmer said, 'I hope they socks have been washed. Got to think of the folk who eat the carn afterwards, see?' I can't remember if they were or not but, knowing me, I can't see myself cutting the feet off of a pair of clean stockings without having a wear of them first!

There was one farm I remember in particular. We had only gone there for the one day's work. The farmer's son was just turned fourteen, had left school, and liked to chuck his orders about to the labourers. I think the farmer encouraged him in this.

'You can go up to . . . !' he started to tell me.

'Ernie's in charge of I!' I informed him. 'Tell him.'

'*I'm* tellin' thee!' he roared back.

'I can hear,' I said. 'Tell Ernie. He'll tell I . . . '

He told Ernie and went off in search of Varmer. We finished the day's work and Varmer came up to Ernie and paid him.

'How much do I pay the bwoy?' he asked Ernie.

'Half-a-crown,' said Ernie.

Varmer held up a half-crown and said to me, 'You can have this if you fight my bwoy for it.'

'Hang on a bit, Varmer,' I shouted. 'I've earnt that money. That's mine!'

'Alright, alright,' he said as he tossed the coin to me, 'I were just havin' a bit of fun, you know.'

Varmer looked very pleased . . . Ernie looked a little downcast . . .

'Can I borrow thy cap, Ernie?' I asked . . . and he complied.

I dropped the cap, inside-upwards, at Varmer's feet. I then tossed the half-crown into the hat.

'There you are, Varmer,' I said. '*My* money!—It says one-and-three I can beat un, and one-and-three he haven't got the guts to take I on!'

Varmer paid another two-and-six without seeing a fight.

I'd beaten the son in two fights when he was at school . . . The first fight was because he had tripped up Thin Norm in the playground. I think the second fight was because he couldn't believe the result of the first fight.

Armour with a Clink in

Vather got a shoe-tack in his eye, and the factory folk sent him straight off to the Eye Hospital up-Bristol . . .

This upset the noisy calm of our family life, somewhat . . . You see, they told us to send on Vather's pyjamas and toilet gear, and Vather didn't have any . . . Our Mother sent me up-town to buy some (red and white striped ones, they were), and, on the following day, I had to catch the first Birstil Bus to deliver them to Vather . . . He could have gone without those pyjamas for all I was bothered . . . Still . . . As Mother pointed out, he was 'feelin' bad', and I couldn't help feeling just a little bit sorry for him, even if he was my father . . .

It was all such a rush . . . Getting the pyjamas . . . Sending the letter to school . . . Catching the bus . . . I didn't have time to size things up . . . I just got on with the next item on hand . . . I didn't think . . .

Bristol was the big city . . .

Bristol was twenty-eight miles away and, on the old Birstil Bus, Bristol was also one hour and forty-five minutes away . . .

We got to Wells (six miles from home), without incident . . . I had been to Wells once before, and I was just as impressed on this occasion as I had been the time before . . . 'It wasn't "home",' I thought . . . From there on-out, it was new ground and, with the passing of each mile, I got a little more apprehensive . . . 'Is this Birstil?' I wondered as each small village or town appeared . . . I couldn't ask the conductor. I didn't know him . . . Then, slowly, the situation dawned on me. I had never been anywhere on my own before. I was 'getting-in' out of my depth! How that bus ride dragged on and on . . . Me in a bus full of people with no one to talk to . . . I began to get worried . . . My getting-off point was easily solved. The gradual build-up of the masses of buildings, busy roads, and traffic was an accumulative warning that I was almost there - . . . and then came the solution . . . The end of the line where everybody got off . . . So blimmin' simple . . . What in the hell had I been worried about, anyroad?

The noise was deafening . . . People shouted here to talk to one another, and not because they had something to shout about . . . Lots

of bustling traffic went anywhere and to nowhere in particular. They
just followed their front wheels, and honked their horns at the folk who
fought to find a space to plant their feet as they jostled from where-
they'd-been to where-they'd-finish-up . . . The buildings were dirty and
tall . . . So tall, their tops leant over to touch one another above the road
. . . All this noise and movement—and I couldn't see or hear a darn thing.

I asked old ladies . . . (you don't ask strange blokes), 'Please, where's
the Eye Hoss-piddle?' Some didn't know, and some would tell me such
a long tale that I would only remember the first bit, and I would politely
listen to the rest without hearing a word . . . and then I'd ask an old
lady . . . And I wanted to 'go' so bad . . . (must have been all that excite-
ment, or summat). I hadn't 'been' since before I left home, and you
can't ask old ladies, 'Please, where's the lavat'ry, Missus?' can you?

Such a dear old lady . . . No, she didn't know where the Eye Hospital
was . . . She knew where the 'Gen'ral' was, though . . . Had her arm done
there, she did . . . Aw, me vather were bad in there, were ur, me love? . . .
Had a tack in his eye, did ur? . . . And where do I come from, love? Aw,
Missus, me dear, what's all that got to do with it?

Trust our Vather to come all up here where nobody can't find un!
Why couldn't he go out Butleigh Hospital like everybody else?

I found it at last . . . Oh, God, it looked too posh for the likes of we.
And how in the hell is it possible not to be able to find a place as big as
this? Only about a mile from where I'd got off the bus! I'd been over
every bit of Birstil, I think. And why shouldn't I keep 'keepin'-on'?—I'd
got a bus to catch-back, s'no. Caw . . . And didn't I want to 'go' real-bad,
too . . .

I walked into the room . . . Vather was sat up in bed with his eye
bandaged up . . . He smiled-sick, and said a tired 'Hullo' . . . The sod
smiled!—And there was he sat up in bed with a nightshirt on! *And*, here
was me, coming all up here, all this time, with some pyjamas what we'd
bought and he didn't want!

Yes, he smiled at me . . . He wanted to tell somebody about how
they'd took his eye out and let it dangle on a string in a silver bowl
while he 'were still lookin'' . . . He wanted to tell somebody all about
the pain and how he'd suffered . . . Anybody with a pair of ears would
have done, and I just happened to be handy . . . And he was worried . . .
He was worried about home . . . 'How's Mam?' he asked. That's *his* Mam,
by the way . . . If he had meant mine, he would have said, 'How's thy
mother?' I didn't know . . . I hadn't seen her . . .

'How's Our Young'un, then?'—And that didn't mean he was interested in one of his many young'uns. He meant his brother. I hadn't seen him, neither, but Mother has sent him some pyjamas . . .

Pyjamas?—What did he want they for?—He didn't never wear they things!

. . . and Mother'd sent him some apples . . .

Apples! She ought to know that he didn't never eat they, neither.

. . . I liked apples, Vather . . .

Ah, yes . . . He knew all about that. He knew I'd like anything, I would . . . He'd hang onto them, he would . . . Might come in handy if he felt like one later on . . .

The nurse came in . . . Was everything alright, Mister Burrows?

Oh, yes . . . Not too bad, considerin', he wasn't . . . but he hadn't half been through it, though . . . He didn't know how he'd managed to stand it all, really, he didn't . . . And look what 'Young Useless', here, had brought him. Pyjamas! . . . and he simpered like a gert big slug in a bowl of chicken bran . . .

The nurse unwrapped the brown paper parcel . . . She thought they were very nice pyjamas . . .

We'd said all we had to say, and I had a bus to catch-back . . .

Was I coming up again?

No. We didn't have enough money.

No money?—What did she do with all the money he'd given her? (Probably squandered it on food for we kids, I thought.) I didn't say nothing. He took his purse from his locker, and held it close to his good eye, and took out a ten-bob note without disturbing the rest of the contents . . . He hesitated . . . He didn't suppose I'd got any change on me, had I? He was dead right, and a warm glow of satisfaction almost forced a smile about my clenched teeth . . . Well, then . . . Have that, and let him have the change . . . if there's any . . . See that?—He knew this boy well . . .

'Tell Mam 'tis a bit dry up here, will 'ee?—And tell her they don't let nobody have cider in here. And tell Our Young'un the same,' won't I?

He gave me one of those sly, fawning, knowing, smirks of his . . . I felt sick.

I took the ten-bob note, and gave him one of my knowing looks . . . Yes, I'd tell them, alright . . .

I left that room unknowingly-knowing what it is like to have been in close contact with a leper . . . They had toilets in the hospital, but I thought they were for the doctors and nurses and the folk in there all the time . . . so I didn't 'go' . . .

I got back to the bus stop in record time and, by now, I was a little
more used to the scrabbling mass of human maggotry . . . and I began
to see . . . I began to realize . . .

At home, we would stand on a given spot to wait for 'the bus', the
'Town Bus'. But what in the hell did I have to do here? There were six
buses in a row where I'd got off . . . There was another row of buses on
the other side of the road . . . I tried to read their names, but they kept
on moving . . . I couldn't read them all, because they didn't give me time!—
And then buses just drove straight through between the rows, and I
didn't have a chance at all . . . Hey! Slow-up for Christ sake!—I might
want to get on! Oh, God . . . Which one was mine?

I tried, and I tried, for hours and hours . . . I was tired . . . I was
hungry . . . I was puggoo'd . . . and this fear of never catching the 'Town
Bus' gave me a thirst of all thirsts . . . Funny . . . Late winter, and I had
a summer thirst . . . and I still wanted to 'go' so bad . . . I saw this alley-
way . . . I went through it and came out into a cobbled stable yard . . . I
staggered to the dung heap . . . got me diddler down me trouser leg . . .
and thanked God for small mercies . . . I thought I was never going to
stop . . . I went back through the alley . . . back to the crowds and shuf-
fling buses . . . Oh, God, I was tired . . . I was hot . . . I was worried . . . I
was thirsty . . .

Hey, hang on a minute . . . Don't get Our Mother wrong, mind. She'd
gave me threepence extra for a cup of tea and a bun. She'd thought of
me, alright . . . But I couldn't go in one of they-Birstil caffs and ask for a
cup of tea and a bun, could I? I mean, it might have cost more than threepence up here.

Damn and blast it . . . I was so tired with all of it, I was . . .

Two men talked as their fully harnessed cart horses drank from a
trough . . . The reins were hung on the hames . . . All coiled up in big
loops, they were . . . Water . . . Just what I wanted, but wait a minute,
though . . . This was the Birstil Hoss Trough. This wasn't our'n . . .

I addressed the older man of the two . . . 'Can I have drink of water,
please, Mister?' The old man studied my face . . . He was serious . . .

'Help yerself, m'son,' he said.

The younger bloke sort of grinned . . . I walked between the two
horses . . . I passed the edge of my hand across the surface of the water
to remove the floating scraps of chaff . . . and as I bent forward to drink,
I saw two water beetles scuttle away about six inches below the surface
. . . Funny . . . I thought . . . Don't never see 'water-skaters' on top of a
hoss trough . . . and I drank greedily . . . The curled-up lapels of my

jacket rested on the surface . . . They rested so light, you'd think they
wouldn't get wet . . . It was cold . . . It was good . . . I finished
drinking . . .

'Drinking from a horse trough!' . . . I suppose somebody's tut-tuttin'
. . . So what?—We'd got our set of safety rules, you know. We weren't
ignorant. 'If horses drink it—it's clean' . . . 'If it's bleeding and dirty, let
the dog lick it clean' . . . and if something else crops up . . . Well . . .
'You've gotta eat a peck o' dirt a'fore you die,' haven't you?

I wasn't thirsty any more . . . The hunger had gone with the thirst . . .
The mare on my right had stopped drinking, and was studying me with
one of the loveliest, loving, brown eyes in the world . . .

'Hello, stranger,' the lovely eye said . . .

'Hello, me lovely,' I replied . . . 'You'm a lovely girl, you be . . . I bet
Our Gramf's hoss would have loved thee, s'no . . . '

I don't know what went wrong but the tears started to come and I
roared like a gert baby . . . I gently cuddled the huge head in my arms,
and pressed my cheek to her forehead.

Sod it . . . Damn you . . . Don't cry!—Not here!!

'Don't cry, m'son,' the old man said . . .

'I bain't cryin' . . . 'Tis just that the Town Bus is a long time, that's
all.'

The Town Bus? . . . What town bus? He knew. 'The Town Bus'.
Where did I come from? . . . Aw, ah . . . *That* town bus . . . He'd see
about it, he would.

I slooshed my face in the trough . . . unbuttoned my jacket, and wiped
my face in the tattered lining . . . I turned to face them, and the old man
had gone . . . The younger man wasn't grinning any more . . .

'Don't worry, young'un . . . We'll see thee alright . . . This place can
be a bit strange to thee, if you don't know . . . '

He took a small apple from his jacket pocket and offered it to me . . .
A cider apple, I thought . . . Kingston Black, by the look of it . . . I bit it
in half . . . Yes, it was a Kingston Black, alright. It put a sort of fur on
your teeth, and had a sort of sweet-bitter taste . . . The bared flesh of
the apple would turn brown before I'd trimmed it down to the core.

'Never eat a hoss's nubbins,' the small, hard-earned, treats . . .

I offered a half to each horse . . . and the younger man showed no
surprise . . .

The older man came back . . . I'd missed one bus . . . (And who wouldn't
Moving them about all the time, like they do up here!) He gave me an
apple . . . A Bramley . . . I thanked him . . . and disposed of it in the

same way . . .

The old man stood me on my bus stop . . . It would definitely stop here . . . I would have to wait a very long time, but not to worry . . . The Town Bus *would* come . . . He gave me a bottle of ginger beer with a marble inside the neck . . . Now, that hurt . . . There was no need . . . I'd got threepence in my pocket . . . I didn't have to mind about that— but would I leave the bottle over by that green tin 'lectric box . . . Yes, I would . . . I thanked him for everything . . . and I could have kicked the legs from beneath him for his extra kindness . . . and he went back to his horse . . .

The ginger beer was soon gone . . . The empty was deposited . . . It *was* a long wait . . . It started to rain . . . one of those light, misty, driz- zly, rains that rests on your clothes like cotton wool and soaks you twice as effectively . . . There was some shelter on the other side of the road, but I wasn't going to leave my bus stop . . . When the bus arrived I was soaked to the skin . . . I gratefully clambered aboard, and settled in my seat . . . A trickle of rainwater ran from my soaking hair . . . I brushed my face with the sleeve of my jacket . . . The rancid smell of horse sweat assailed my nostrils, and I pressed my face into the soaking- wet air of comfort . . . 'Hello, stranger' . . . Hello . . . Hello . . . Hello . . . We'd met before, anyroad!

The bus driver didn't know the way straight-home. Chased all over the place, he did . . . We pulled up in-town, and I was off like a shot . . . I ran across the Market Place . . . down past the church . . . past the Police Station, and didn't look back until I got to a field . . . I climbed the railings . . . ran through the field . . . rushed across the next one . . . and then sat breathless up-top a gate post with my feet resting on the top rail of the gate . . .

No one for miles around . . . and I didn't feel lonely any more . . . Ever feel like shouting at nothing, did 'ee? I have . . . and did . . . using every swear word of affection I could lay my tongue to.

'How's yer vather?' Our Mother wanted to know.

'Alright,' I said.

'What did ur say to thee?'

'Nothin' much,' I told her. 'He sent thee ten bob.'

'*He* sent *I* ten bob?!—That bad eye of his must've gone to his head!'

I told Gran and Uncoo what Our Vather had told me . . .

'We shall have to send un on a drop o' whisky, then,' said Gran.

'Won't be much good, Gran,' I told her, 'they don't like booze in hoss-piddle.'

'But they wouldn't know if you took it in,' Uncoo said.

'I dunno about that,' I said, 'but that nurse even unwrapped his pyjamas what I took up for un.'

'She didn't, did she?' they both said.

Vather's face had the same look as when I'd left him . . . A nauseating, friendly smile . . . and I knew he detested relying on me, as much as I disliked his false friendliness . . .

Had I seen Mam? . . . Yes I had . . . And had I seen his Young'un? . . . Yes I had . . . And what had um sent him?

'Nothin', Vather. They said they'd buy thee a drink when you'm home.'

'Didn't nobody send I nothin'?'

'No . . . Still got all they apples, though, haven't 'ee?'

'Blimmin' young'uns of t'day. Can't do nothin' properly! . . . And I, in here, with me bad eye . . . Well, get on home, then, if you haven't got nothin' sensible to say! Tell thy mother I shall be comin' home this weekend . . . '

I walked past the bus stop . . . The Town Bus was in, but it wasn't important . . . I could catch the next one . . . I entered the stable yard . . . and there they were . . . all together . . . the cart-horses were still hitched up to their waggons . . .

'Hullo, Mister. Can I give um some nubbins, please?' . . . and I held up the big bag of Blenheim fall-downs (they could still be found if the orchard grass was long enough).

'Ah, alright, m'son, but not all-they, mind . . . Still got some work to do, see?'

I gave the horses two apples each . . . and I hugged the mare's head once more again.

'Thanks very much, Mister,' I said.

He looked through my face once again . . .

''Tis the hoss-sweat what do do it,' he said. 'Make folks eyes water, it do.'

'Ah, it do, alright,' I agreed. 'Shall I leave the rest of these apples in the oat-bin, Mister?'

'Ah. Thee do that, m'son . . . '

'And I've got a bottle of cough-mixture for the horse . . . Shall I leave that there, as well?'

'Cough-mixture?—Ah. Do that, m'son . . . And thanks very much . . . '

'Pleasure, Mister . . . and don't mind about the bottle . . . '

I entered the unfamiliar stable . . . I placed the apples in the bin . . . I removed Vather's quart bottle of cider from the bag, and placed it beside the apples . . . See . . . Had Vather come home that night, instead of going to the hospital, he would have drunk it before going up-town to consume his daily, or nightly, quota. Sort of a primer, it was . . . He'd drank the other quart before going to work . . . and I had put a drop of paraffin in the bottom of that empty bottle . . .

I walked back into the light of the dim stable yard . . . They were leaving by the alley . . . The mare didn't look back, or whinney . . . The old man waved at me, though . . . I walked out of that barton (yard) feeling ten-foot tall . . . All square, all round . . . I didn't never know his name . . . I didn't know her'n, neither . . .

It makes you think, doesn't it? The only foster-mother I'd ever had . . . and I didn't know her name.

More and More Schooldays

I had now arrived in 'Sir's' class and Our Young'un was in the first 'Miss's' class (poor devil), but here I was, going back to see 'Miss' after school.

It was Our Mother's fault, really. She had told me to inform 'Miss' that Our Young'un couldn't come to school because it was raining and he had holes in his boots. I told 'Miss' he was feeling bad.

'Alright, Ray-dream,' she said. 'We didn't dream that little lot up, did we?'

How I hated her. It was fine in the afternoon and Our Young'un came back to school, but I forgot to tell him what had been wrong with him—hence the after-school visit.

'Why didn't you tell me the truth?' she asked.

Telling her he wasn't coming—that's her business. Holes in his boots—that's family!

'Don't know, Miss,' I said.

'I have told you before. If you tell lies you will always get found out, didn't I?'

With a brother like him—it's bound to happen! Well? What was she going to do now that she knew the truth? Buy him a new pair of boots?

'Yes, Miss,' I said.

'Very well then. Go to the headmaster and tell him why I have sent you to him.'

Off I went. Getting caned after school now!—They'd be doing it at home before very long. I crossed the playground to his classroom . . . I bet myself she was watching me through the window. I knocked the door with the ring-handle.

'Come in,' he shouted-through, and I entered the almost empty classroom.

'Hullo, Sir,' I said. 'Would you like I to put some books away, or summat?'

'What have you been sent here for?' he thundered. I ask you—how did he know?

Two on each hand . . . Not too bad, I suppose.

'Did you say you were sorry?' he asked . . . and I hadn't.

'Are you going to?' he asked . . . and I wasn't.

'And why not?'

''Cos I've just been caned for it, Sir.'

'Well then—you had better have a couple more for sulking.'

'But, Sir,' I said, 'I didn't mean *because* I've just been caned. I meant, because I didn't ought to be tellin' any more lies!'

'Then I shall have to punish you for being ungracious and stubborn. Hold out your hand.'

('Oh, do thee stop nudgin' the back of my hand with that cane, Sir,' I thought. 'Just tell me where you want it . . . Up or down . . . I can hold it there meself, thank you.')

Our Mother said I wouldn't go Heaven. She also said the District Nurse brought the babies in her little black bag—and I worked on a farm! Still, she could believe what she liked, I suppose. It was a free country, wasn't it?

I was sat in the classroom when the headmaster came in with a smile as wide as the doorway. We were lucky. Our headmaster was always laughing and joking about something. He spoke in muttered undertones to 'Sir' and they both looked in my direction and smiled.

'Your younger brother hasn't brought his football boots today,' the headmaster informed me in front of my classmates. 'He says he has lost them somewhere in the pantry at home. That's a funny place to keep football boots, isn't it?'

'Not really, Sir,' I replied. 'He's on about the pantry with the shelfs-in under the stairs, but 'tis all damp and "mowdy" in there, so we don't keep any grub in there—just things like the washing, old clothes, and toys—and football boots.'

That blimmin' young'un!—Always landing me in it, he was. He never seemed to care *what* he said! Being poor, and knowing it—there's nothing wrong with that, and it's nothing to be ashamed of . . . But it isn't something to be so blatantly proud of neither! . . . Blimmin' brother.

Going home from school that evening, I carefully planned my to-morrow.

'What have 'ee got for tea tonight?—Fried football boots?' (I'll get him . . .)

'How about a drop of shoe-lace soup then?' (. . . and him . . .)

'Ever tried a football-sock sangwich?' (. . . and him as well!)

The headmaster asked me on the later part of the tomorrow,

'Why do I have to keep on caning you?' (You bloody well know, Laughin' Gas!)

'Don't know, Sir,' I replied.

On another occasion the headmaster came into the classroom with his cane in his hand.

'Come out here!' he said.

'What me?' I wondered . . . 'Yes, you!' he looked back . . . so out I went . . .

'Hold out your hand,' he said.

'What for, Sir?' I asked.

'Hold out your hand. I shan't tell you again!'

'But, Sir,' I said. 'I haven't done nothin'.'

'Come on, now. We don't usually have this silly trouble. For the last time. Hold out your hand!'

'Alright, Sir, but I haven't been fightin', or nothin'.' (Not that I could remember, anyroad.) Three on each hand . . . That was the same as for fighting . . . Must have been something I had forgotten about . . . something from a while-back. The thighs of my grey flannel trousers had only just erased the smarting from my palm and fingers when the headmaster re-entered the classroom.

'Come out here!' he said.

This wasn't my day . . . I might forget one thing, but not two! I did as I was ordered. He observed my consternation—and then burst into laughter.

'I'm sorry about that caning just now,' he said. 'It wasn't you, it was your brother!'

Do you see what I mean about his sense of humour? You may not believe this, but I didn't feel too badly about it. You see, 'Losers don't get caned.' Our Young'un was coming on!

A few days later, I was contemplating during a lull in the class routine. Prayers had been said in record time and teacher's pet was handing out the corrected sum books. I studied the paper-flighted pen nibs stuck into the high beams on the ceiling and tried to make patterns from the blue-black dollops of dried-out blotting paper on the ceiling between the beams . . .

. . . and the headmaster came in with his cane.

I looked at the standard Somerset County Committee wall clock. Nine-fifteen . . . Five minutes later than usual . . . He must have been having a busy morning . . .

'Come out here,' he said, and I obeyed with alacrity.

'We know what this is for, don't we?' he said.

'Yes, Sir.'

'Right. Hold out your hand.'

'But, Sir,' I said. 'You caned I for nothin' last time!'

'Well?' he said. 'And I said I was sorry, didn't I?'

'Yes, Sir,' I replied, 'and I'm sayin' "sorry" now, Sir.'

'And did you say sorry to the other boy?'

'Well, not exactly, Sir, 'cos we ain't sort of talkin' to one another for a while, but I will later on, Sir.'

'That's not the same thing, is it?' he replied. 'Hold out your hand!'

I could have sworn I was onto a good thing there, s'no. I held out my hand to keep him in his good-humoured self. Strange . . . I always respected him though, and I don't think he would have got my respect without that cane. No . . . It wasn't *just* his sense of humour . . .

Folk Lessons

I was in the barton alongside the stalls loading a putt with dung.

Into the yard came a man with one arm and he backed his putt alongside mine. His huge grey made Old Mooch look like a foal stood beside him. Both of them worked for a local builder and it looked as though the builder was intending to do some gardening.

I was young enough to feel my feet and was beginning to realize I was perty good with a pick and dung fork.

'Can I give thee a hand, Twister?' I asked.

'Whoffor?' was the gruff reply.

'Dunno,' I said. 'Just thought I'd offer.'

'Oh, did 'ee?' he said. He looked into my quarter-full putt. 'Here's tuppence' . . . and he placed the two coins on the top of the low wall.

'I'll bet thee that against a pint of cider that I can fill my putt before you finish filling thine!'

The miserable old devil. I'd show him! I took him on . . . I went like the wind, I did, and, when I had finished in record time, Twister was sat on the wall . . . waiting . . . and the tuppence had disappeared. I went and asked Varmer for a bottle of cider. He laughed, because he knew I didn't drink it.

'Been trying to take tuppence off of Old Twister, have 'ee?' he said. 'T'would take a good bloke to beat he, let I tell thee!'

Over the next couple of years I got to be much better and faster and I had another three attempts at beating Twister. It cost me four bottles of cider, all told.

T'would take a good bloke to beat him, Varmer had said. T'would take a blimmin' good bloke to keep up with him! Still—a little more time, lots-more practice . . . and one day . . .

As Twister said as he drank my fourth bottle of cider, 'You'm gettin' better 'n' betterer, Young'un. Thee go a bit faster next time and I 'spect you'll perty-nigh make I start "pankin'"' (panting).

I entered the barn to find Old Joe sorting out the sack bags 'ready for sendin' back'. He was placing them in three piles. Joe looked after the horses and carts. Funny how it was almost always a little man who did that job. Did the horses appreciate smaller folk?

'Can I give thee a hand, Joe?' I asked.

'Ah, if you'm minded, me son. Mind how you go though, 'cos there only used to be two kinds and now there be three . . . Got somebody else sendin' us stuff, now, I s'pose . . . '

I got stuck into the job . . .

'Here, Joe, there's only two kinds—Birch's and Phipps's.'

'Oh, is there?—What about they new uns there, then?'

'They be Phipps's as well, but they've been done a different way, and they'm red instead of black—like they be usually. Can't you read, Joe?'

'Well . . . Not a lot, I can't . . . Thought I *were* readin' alright for the last ten year or so—and then they do go and change the colour of um! . . . Can't leave nothin' alone, can um?'

'But how do you get on if you can't read, Joe?'

'Hoy, here!' he replied. 'What do 'ee mean, how do *I* get on? Why do a putt tip?'

''Cos he's a bit-off from middle on the axle, and he "goes" when you let off the handle up-front.'

'Oh? . . . And why don't ur slop all-up-round the horse's rear when they'm goin' downhill?'

''Cos of the bum-band on the brichin' . . . Horse do take the weight on his haunches, and you can use the break a bit, as well.'

'Well, well, well . . . And *who* told thee that?'

'Thee!'

'Not bad for a bloke what can't read, is it?'

'Ohhhh, sorry, Joe. I didn't mean it like that. Honest.'

'Sorry?—Don't thee be sorry, me son. I don't mind not writin' and readin'—I'd like to, but I ain't sorry about it. What would 'ee do if Mooch went down sudden with cholic—bad?'

'Dunno, Joe . . . What would you?'

'I'd send for the vet, 'cos he do know better than I! See—how I do look at it, is . . . It don't matter *how many* things you do know about, it ain't no good to thee if you haven't got nobody *to tell it to*. See what I mean, do 'ee? If everybody know'd everything, folk wouldn't have nothin' to talk about—apart from the weather, perhaps . . . How long do 'ee think 'tis goin' to stay fine for?'

'Dunno, Joe, do I?'

An educated bloke, was Joe—and he could teach.

'Ever been hurt by a cart-horse, Joe?' I asked.

'No, can't say I have . . . Always move steady . . . Always move sure
. . . It ain't the nastiness of a horse, 'tis the frightenin' of him what does
it.'

'Ain't none of um natural-nasty then, Joe?'

'No. All done by kindness, 'tis . . . Kindness 'n' trust . . . They'm
what *you* make um . . . Bigger the beast, the more gentler they be.'

'Is that Jonick, Joe?'

'Of course 'tis. Have you ever heard of anybody round here what
have been clunked by a bad-tempered elephant?'

No, I hadn't . . . Joe was quite right there . . . Hey, hang on a mo'!—
I'd only seen six of them in my life! 'Here, Joe . . . ' I said. Joe had
turned away from me. He was standing, head down, holding a broken
bridle. His shoulders were 'humptied-up' and they did seem to 'bumpty-
quiet'. He was having a quiet laugh. That Joe had 'been on with his nonsense' with me!

'No, Joe, I haven't never heard of nothin' like that,' I said, 'and
come-to-think, I haven't never heard of anybody what have been bit by
a shark when the floods were out, neither!'

Joe's silent titter exploded into laughter. He handed me a pocket-worn
pop-bag.

'Well done, me son,' he laughed. 'Here. You can have these two jubes.
I were goin' to give um to Mooch, but she won't mind.'

I took them with thanks, and gave them to Mooch. I was fond of
those sweets but that horse had a dozen ways of looking at you which
could make the tastiest of morsels taste like sawdust.

There was also the time when Joe eyed the furrow I had just completed with the horses and plough. He wasn't 'learning' me properly
because I was too young. He was just letting me have a go. With Samp-
son and Mooch hitched up there was nothing wrong with the team.
There was nothing wrong with the plough, but something wasn't quite
right, somewhere . . .

'Bit of a wobble just up-top of the "knap", ain't there, me son?'

'Ah, I have zig-zagged a bit there, Joe,' I admitted.

'Zig-zag?' said Joe. 'That ain't a zig-zag, me son. That's a wobble if
ever I've seen one . . . A bit of stone and clay, there is, up there . . . You
didn't allow enough "right-elbow"—but it ain't a zig-zag, is it?'

'Well . . . Both the same, ain't um?'

'Course it ain't! If they'm the same, why call um different? That's a
wobble. Now thee tell I . . . What's a zig-zag? Why not call un a "zag-zig",
or a "zig-zig", or a "zag zag"? Come on, now. Thee tell I what a "zig" or

a "zag" is!'

'Well . . . If t'were a clothes line, he's "zig" on the sides and "zag" in the middle . . . '

'That ain't what I said. "Zig" and "zag" on-the-flat, I do want!'

'Well . . . This way's "zig" (right) . . . and back t'other way (left) . . . is "zag".'

'And what if you'm cack-handed?'

''Tis all the same for they, too!'

'Oh, all the same, is it?—Then what about comin' back?—Thy "zigs" would be "zags" then, wouldn't um—and I haven't never heard of a "zag-zig", have you?'

'No, Joe, I haven't . . . Alright, I s'pose 'tis a wobble up-top then!'

'The trouble with thee is—for all that learnin' they've give thee, you don't know your wobbles from your zig-zags, do 'ee?'

'No, I don't, Joe . . . '

'—And I'll tell thee summat else, young feller-me-lad. You don't know your zigs from your zags, neither!'

What could I say? He was right—I didn't know any more.

'I were wrong there, Joe,' I said.

'No. You weren't *wrong*, me son (but that *is* a wobble, mind). Young'uns have got to say things like that so's we old uns can tell um right. Thee listen, like what you've just been doin', and you can grow to be a big man without growin' tall—*or*—you can finish up being humble all thy life! Young'uns's questions do keep we old folk *YOUNG*, s'no.'

'Do um, Joe?'

'Ah, they do. And all this talkin' have just put years on I!'

It didn't show, Joe . . . It didn't show . . .

I was cutting some chaff when little Old Perce came up to me in a rush as usual.

Folk said Perce wasn't very bright because he couldn't add, read, or write, but I have still to meet the bloke who could get a halfpenny, a cigarette, or free drink out of him. He always had some little thing to tell me and I would always listen because the small things in life seemed so important to him. This item was much bigger than usual though.

'Have 'ee heard about they two old folk who come back from their holidays and got robbed and beated up?' he asked.

'No, I haven't, Perce. From round here, be um?'

'No. They'd been on holiday. Haven't 'ee heard?'

'No, Perce. Don't read the papers much, I don't.'

'T'weren't in they. T'were on the wireless.'

'Don't never listen to he a lot nowadays, neither, Perce.'

'Ah. These two old folk went on their holidays and, when they come back, they young blokes beated um up summat-cruel and took all their money off of um!'

'Get on?'

'Ah. It ain't good enough, is it?'

'No, it ain't, Perce.'

'I mean—they old folk have got a nice little home there, and it ain't no business of they young blokes if they old folk had been on their holidays, is it?'

'It ain't, Perce.'

'Well . . . They got rights to go away if they want to—and they can come back again to their own home without t'others hittin' um and robbin' um!'

'They *can*, Perce.'

'Somebody ought to do the same thing to they!—And give um a good hidin' as well, didn't um?'

'Ah, they did.'

'Ah. Give um a good hidin', and then take um up Police Station and summons um!'

'Ah . . .'

'Ah. Give um a good hidin' . . . Take um up Police Station . . . Summons um, and then give um a good "drashin'".'

'Ah, that's about *it*, Perce.'

'Ah. About time thiick cat 'n' nine tails were brung back . . . Give um a good hidin' . . . Take um up Police Station . . . Summons um . . . Give um a good drashin' with the cat 'n' nine tails, and rub some salt in!'

'Oh, Ah, Perce . . . Musn't forget the salt.'

'Ah. Put lots of salt on and rub it in ever so hard, and . . . well . . . Hangin' is too good for they, ain't it?

''Tis, Perce.'

'No . . . No good hangin' um if 'tis too quick . . . Rub some more salt in and make um bide and wait . . . Hangin' *do* kill um quick, don't it?'

'It *do*, Perce.'

'Ah. Give um a good hidin' . . . Take um up Police Station and summons um . . . Give um the cat 'n' nine tails and rub lots and lots of salt in ever so hard—and then put um under the *GELATINE*! Ah, that's what they ought to do, didn't um?'

'Ah, they did, Perce. Make um go like jelly!'
It was hard work, but I didn't laugh. Well, I couldn't, could I?
As I told you—the little things in life were important to Perce.

Growing Pains...

I was just gone twelve when I experienced my first physical attempt at open rebellion against the grown-ups. I could move quickly, was strong for my age, and had a quick temper which seldom left me with enough time for prolonged arguments.

We were stealing Morgan Sweets from Jimmy Mapsone's orchard. There were a lot of soft, pappy apples on the ground, but I was up in the tree tossing down the firmer, juicier apples to my younger brothers who were stowing them inside their shirts.

There was a shout of 'Watch out!' I jumped down and we all rushed to the gap in the hedge. In the middle of the hedge was a wire fence and I had pointed this out to the young'uns.

'Don't try to jump it or climb over it,' I had told them. 'Don't try to stand on it neither—just put your foot on the top stretch and keep runnin'.'

The dog went through at a lope . . . Young'un (next one down) cleared it like a gazelle . . . I went through and, as I paused to help Young'un (two down) if the need arose, there was a shriek like the noise of a snared rabbit and the dog snarled and turned immediately. I grabbed her by the collar, and there, on the other side of the gap, was Dan'l, the farm labourer, holding Our Young'un by the scruff of the neck. He had dropped some of his apples and had stopped to pick them up! Why hadn't I thought of that?

Dan'l was a well-built man of about thirty years old. Why was he interfering?—They weren't his apples, he only worked on the farm!

'Leave un be, Mister!' I demanded without realizing I was addressing the whole race of the persecuting grown-ups. The look of victory dropped from Dan'l's face like a wet sack on a stone floor. He eyed me apprehensively. Perhaps he doubted that I could hold the snarling Airedale. I could see fear in his eyes. Grown-ups could be afraid.

'Right, Young Swiggy, thy vather shall hear about this,' said Dan'l. 'Now clear off out of it, the lot of thee, and don't let I catch thee again!'

I had more than my fair share of boyhood fights—where the blows were

162

the blows of children, just strong and hard enough to bloody the nose, lips, and knuckles. The only fights I remember were the ones that had a special incident attached to them.

Take the fight with Cocker, for instance. We 'lathered' one another from the Police Station . . . up around Grope Lane behind Saint Benedict's church . . . and then all along the length of 'The Tins' (a long narrow footpath with a fence of corrugated-iron sheets on one side), and there the cheering, jeering mob of the usual junior fight-followers declared it a draw. Nothing out of the ordinary but, during our stormy passage through Grope Lane some dear old lady threw a white enamelled bucket of water over us (was it water?)—It came from the upstairs window, anyroad.

There was the baffling Duck who had been taught to box properly by his father. He beat me every time he could get me to lose my temper—which was every time. I had a few sessions with Cully who was bigger and older but had learnt to box and was only too pleased to demonstrate, using me as a punch bag. Fighting was already becoming a science to me.

I awoke early, as usual, and arose to get ready to go work. I yawned and stretched . . . Something was wrong!

'Mother!—I can't see!' (This is a first-class way to wake someone up.)

During my slumbers, blood had trickled from my recently broken nose and had congealed on my eye-lids. This incident frightened me, but not half as much as it frightened Our Mother when she came into the bedroom and saw me!

I was horsing about with the dog just outside Our Gran's.

Awver, a man about the same age as Our Vather, was working in his allotment on the other side of the road and was just putting the finishing touches to the raking of his seed bed. Some stupid cat suddenly sighted Our Dog and ran across Awver's seed bed with Tacks closely following like a juggernaut with the fly.

Awver didn't like dogs, especially our'n.

He didn't like kids—and he hated me. It was Awver who reported me to Varmer Clark, informing him that I had been trying to catch one of his hares—a silly, nasty, spiteful thing to do, because everybody was trying to catch one of them. I wasn't doing so, of course, but I *had* sent the dog after it. I wasn't stupid.

As Tacks sped across the smooth patch of soil Awver recovered from his initial surprise and annoyance at the sudden appearance of the cat, and took a swing at Tacks with his rake, which, had it connected, would have put umpteen stitches in her back. He missed and, before he could reassess the situation, I charged into him stomach-high with my head well down. He fell flat on his back and one of his boots shot out to take the skin from the length of my shin. I was already furious—and now the pain and the indignation of being kicked in the leg by a grown-up! I dived and grabbed for the fallen rake . . . rolled out of reach of Awver . . . and regained my feet . . .

A firm arm encircled my body holding my arms and the rake tightly to me. Another rough, gentle hand covered my cheek and pressed my face against the owner's weskit which comfortingly smelled of earth and stale tobacco.

'Lorr love thee, me dear. You don't want to comb Awver's hair with his own rake, do 'ee?' I heard Old Regg'o's voice asking me.

Awver was shouting excitedly from the seated position. Was I going to strike him with the rake? Was I merely moving it out of reach of the man who had kicked me? I don't know . . .

Vather came out from Gran's . . . He unbuckled his belt . . .

'Let I have he, Reg,' he said. 'I'll soon show he . . . '

'Ah, I'll let thee have un,' said Regg'o, 'but thee touch he with that strap of thine and you'll need that young'un to help carry thee home!'

Tacks had returned . . . just waiting . . .

'Awver,' continued Regg'o. 'Shut thy noise and get on-in-house out-the-way. Thiick dog don't like the look of thee.'

Awver went . . . without a word . . . forgetting his rake in his hurry. Vather pointed it out that it was I who had upset Awver in the first place.

'This young'un were lookin'-out for his dog. Awver tried to rake un!' Old Regg'o thundered.

'But 'tis my bwoy!' Vather insisted.

'Oh, you know that, do 'ee?—I didn't think you ever bemembered.'

'Come here . . . ' Vather said to me. 'Go on home and get to bed. I'll see thee later on . . . '

'Ah, do as thy vather tells thee, me dear,' agreed Regg'o. 'AND,' he added to Vather, 'thee touch one hair of thiick bwoy for what he've done here, and I'll see that you go to bed for a very long time!'

Vather forgot all about it and never mentioned the incident again.

I also remember that Sunday tea time . . . It was also another apple-time in Jimmy's orchard and we had stewed apple and custard with our bread and jam. Vather got up and came down after sleeping his Sunday morning session off. He was his usual good self. He pushed one of the young'uns off his chair in order to sit himself at the table and, with a simultaneous outward sweep of both arms, he cleared a space wide enough for three of him.

'Where's me dinner?' he bellowed to Mother who was out in the back-house warming the big brown enamelled tea-pot. Mother came in with the dinner and knife and fork and placed them on the table in front of him. That dinner had been a dinner at dinner time, but it had been placed in the oven for safe-keeping and had been warmed for about half an hour before he hollered for it. The roast lamb, cabbage, and boiled potatoes had been covered with a generous helping of floury gravy which had been baked crisp around the outsides of the plate. He always ate his Sunday dinner like this.

Why were we eating custard and he didn't never get any of it, he wanted to know.

Because he said he didn't like it . . . He didn't never ask for it . . . and get on with his dinner before it got cold, Mother told him.

He smashed the plate and the dinner in the fireplace. He wanted a cup of tea . . . of course. The cup of tea with no saucer quickly followed the dinner into the fireplace. He wanted another cup of tea with 'not so much sugar in' and why had the milk gone sour? (It had been alright until it met him.) Mother came in with another cup of tea. She bumped the cup down in front of him and, before ripples had reached the rim of the cup, up came the other hand loaded with the boiler stick to deal Vather a sharp rap on the nut! Drink his tea and shut up, she told him. She didn't have the time, money, or the crockery to put up with his tantrums. She didn't inform him that she was probably a little short of patience at that particular moment, but Vather probably realized this.

'You bloody bitch!' he roared and went for Mother.

I met him half-way with a good solid thump to the lower ribs.

('Always catch um off guard. Get in the first punch and make it a good un.')

Vather reeled, clawing at the air as he tried to regain his balance against the bum-high fireguard. Many was the time I had wished him in Hell, but I didn't want him burning all over our clean fireplace. I yanked him from his point of unbalance to a more convenient bend in my direction , and let him have another good one in the eye. He fell between the armchair and the sewing-machine by the window. God, this was easy . . .

('When you get t'other bloke goin', keep un goin'.')

I moved in . . . into a flurry of blows from the boiler stick!

(' . . . and if you'm winnin'—look out for his mates!')

Why had she done that?—I was looking-out for her! I had looked as though I was enjoying it, I was informed.

Mother told me to sit down . . . I sat.

'Don't thee ever do that again!' said Vather from a safely-distanced crooked-finger.

'If I do, I'll kill thee!' I thought. I didn't say nothing.

We weren't allowed to answer back in our house.

Each fight was a lesson. Lessons, seldom remembered—but never forgotten . . .

Games for the 'Old Enough'

In my early teens I used to go up-town to play with Tubb, Ticker, and the rest of the gang. In the evenings of the light-nights our games took us far afield over the surrounding moor. Ditch-jumping was a favourite pastime. An imaginary straight line would be drawn up and we would jump anything in our path—use of the old moor folk vault pole was optional.

We were young . . . We were agile and the odd rhine, ditch, barbed-wire fence and brimble hedge was no problem to us, so we would attempt to put each other off whilst jumping. When someone eventually met their downfall it tended to cool the others for a while until the jibes, taunts and jeers forced the better and the more-foolish to attempt the more impossible. The successes were then applauded, or envied, and the failures were greeted with the laughter they deserved.

In the winter of the dark-nights we would hang about the town. This was when we would play a game of hide and seek and, more often than not, this would take place in the Abbey Ruins. There is an easy access to this hallowed place up over the public lavatories beside the car park.

Before I enter into the mysteries of our game, I would like to point out an additional factor. There were ghosts in the Abbey Ruins. There were ghosts all around the town. Not that I believed in them, mind, but I didn't like to hear about them never the less. It was dead-creepy in the Abbey Ruins at night and took very little imagination to let the mind run riot.

As I told you, hide and seek could be a very rough game. Three would seek to find those who had hidied and, on finding a hider, they would lather him unmercifully until they had procured his promise to stay-put whilst they looked for the others. The promise was always kept.

The Abbey Ruins are a place of the dead. As everyone knows, its end was a violent one, and this is one of the places where King Arthur is buried. 'ONE OF THE PLACES?' you ask. 'Are there more? How can this be?'

I shall show you.

The Glastonbury Abbey Ruins is the rightful place of King Arthur's

grave. We all know this. We know, because we *know*. It is situated in a
patch of lawn. It looks like the rest of the lawns in the Abbey Ruins—
apart from a sign which denotes that spot as the burial place. A most
unimposing sight for the grave of a great king. It looks even less impos-
ing on a winter's night when one is frantically trying to hide from three
blokes who are going to 'lather the hide off of thee' when they find you.

'No. No!' I thought . . . 'A king,' I thought, should have a statue, a
stone-carved tomb or, at least, a hole in the ground.' There being a shortage of un-named statues and uncarved-stone tombs in the area, I settled
for the latter. It was a sort of walled-pit come-entrance come-trench
which reminded me of the secret doors to the pyramids—complete with
a galvanized-wire gate and a padlock to repel all disbelievers. Thus . . .
Armed with a battery of various reasons to answer a variety of disbeliev-
ing questions, King Arthur was restlessly laid to rest in two places in the
Abbey Ruins.

I was 'seeking' and I saw a movement down in King Arthur's new
tomb.

'Is that thee, Tubb?' I asked (because we were special friends).

'Ah, 'tis,' replied Tubb. 'Give us a hand, will 'ee? I think the sides are
a bit too high-up for I to get out.'

'But what be you doin' down in there, anyroad?' I said. 'That's King
Arrter's tomb, s'no!'

'It ain't, is it!?'

'Ah, I think so, me son . . . Hang on a minute, I'll have a look at the
sign . . . Ah! That's right. He's buried down in there alright!'

I flipped a small stone down into the tomb . . . It rattled . . .

Lying toad!—He said he couldn't get out of that hole!

I expect King Arthur had a quiet laugh as well. I expect he thought
to himself, 'My folk can still move when the spirit moves um!'

And what about the time when Jack and Harold came to play with us
for the first time? They had to seek, and you have to split up to do this
in order to cover more ground. That place made Jack very nervous . . .

I had found a good place to hide close to the Abbot's Kitchen. I had
gone up-around some stone steps and had re-emerged on the top of a
wall about six feet from the ground. There was a gert big dark arch above
and behind me . . . It was moonlight . . . I waited . . . I heard someone
coming . . . This wasn't hard to do, because he was shouting-quietly in a
hoarse whisper . . .

'Arroooood . . . ' 'Arrrooooooooood . . . '

It was Jack wishing for Harold.

I wore a long blue scarf. I took it off and placed it over my head to resemble the cowl of a monk. As Jack drew level with my feet, I said,

'I am the ghost of Abbot Whitin' . . . '

Jack stopped . . . and looked slowly up at me in the darkened archway . . . He turned and started to walk away . . . so slowly . . . He hadn't gone three paces when he fell onto his hands and knees . . . and started to crawl . . . ever so slowly . . . I jumped down and tapped him on the shoulder.

'Be you alright, Jack?' I asked.

Jack's arms folded up and he stopped there . . . Head in the grass . . . Tail up . . . It took us ages to bring him round. It frightened me to death! I said to him afterwards,

'You don't believe in Abbot Whitin's ghost down here, do 'ee?'

'Well,' said Jack, 'When I looked up and saw thiick monk and he told I that he were a ghost, it didn't matter to I *who's* ghost he were. I weren't goin' to argue with un! Don't Abbot Whitin's ghost come down here, then?'

'No! Course he don't!' I said. 'He do bide up-Tor!'

We were up-top-the-Tor for New Year's Eve. This is when Abbot Whiting's ghost appears and walks around the tower twelve times . . .

We waited . . . It was bitter-cold . . .

Bong . . . Bong . . . (The clock was striking midnight.)

'Cooh! I ain't half cold,' I said.

'Keep quiet, will 'ee?'

Bong . . . Bong . . .

'Ain't you cold, then?'

'Oh, do thee bide quiet!'

'Ah! Shut thy mouth, will 'ee?'

Bong . . . Bong . . .

'I bet you'm scared. You'm scared, ain't 'ee?'

'No, I ain't! Keep quiet!'

'What's that?'

Bong . . . Bong . . .

'Dunno . . . Didn't hear nothin', did you?'

'No, don't think so . . . '

'Don't think I did, neither.'

Bong . . . Bong . . .

'Cooh! DO—THEE—BIDE—QUIET!'

Bong . . . Bong . . .

All was quiet for a moment. Too quiet for my liking! The cold wind
was tired . . . Too tired to go around you, so it went straight through . . .
It started coming on to another scad of rain . . . No one came . . .

'He ain't goin' to come, s'no,' I said.

'No, I don't think he is,' said Ticker. 'He've got more sense than we've
got—hangin' about in this cold weather! Dunch idear in the first place,
t'were!'

. . . so we came on home . . .

Our Mother was wild, and wanted to know where I had been this
time of the night.

'Up-Tor to see Abbot Whitin',' I said.

'Up-Tor to see . . . ? What do 'ee want to see *he* for?'

'I just wanted to see un, Mother . . . Haven't never seen un before . . . '

'And what did ur say to thee?'

'Nothin', Mother. He didn't come out.'

'Didn't ur? But he *always* comes out on New Year. That's his time!'

'Well, he didn't this time, Mother.'

'Can't understand it . . . He do always come New Year's Eve . . . Still . . .
Only to be expected, I s'pose . . . I 'spect he saw you-lot waitin' to gawp
at un and thought the better of it.'

'We only wanted to see un, Mother . . . We kept quiet . . . '

'Oh, blimmin' young'uns! I don't know what you'm comin' to. I
just don't any more! The only night that poor feller do come out, and
he've got to stay in 'cos you'm up there moochin' about! I 'spect he've
been lookin' forward to that all-year-round, poor devil . . . Happy blimmin'
New Year this is goin' to be for I, I must say! Oh! Get on! Get thyself
to bed out of me sight!'

'Alright, Mother . . . Sorry . . . G'night, Mother . . . '

I lay snug in bed and listened to the wind and rain as it hammered
against the window panes. For over an hour, I fought against the soothing
drug of sleep. I love a storm and this was a luxury too good to miss. I
smiled to myself as I remembered the time when I quietly carried the
bunch of white horse daisies down through Aunt Ider's passage and
rested them against her kitchen door. We then hid under the hedge of
the house on the other side of the road. We sniggered when we heard her
shriek and the tangled mass of flowers flew out of the door into the
gutter. We laughed fit to bust when we saw the silver knife, fork and
spoon appear on the window sill at the partly opened window 'to keep
the devil away' . . .

Superstitious old fool!

'Moor Jumpin'' was also a game we played in the early winter evenings, though not as often as we did in the summer months, because the cold water in those ditches could prove a bit of a beterrent at times.

Regardless of whatever path we chose to return from the moor (and there were dozens of them), our main point of exit was at the end of the Moor Road by Station Lamp. Beside the Railway Station and at the end of the Moor Road is a big house (it used to be a Railway Hotel), and the huge garden to this house had a tall wooden fence surrounding it. This was where we would ritually perform the ceremony of 'Piddlin' a puddle by Weden's Fence'.

Whilst out-in the moor, we would all automatically and self-consciously 'save' in order to be on one's best form at this juncture. We would each select a knot-hole—which was not as easy as it sounds because there were favourite knot-holes and to possess one of them was not a case of first come, first served, but necessitated repelling all boarders who would gallantly attack in ones, twos, and even threes. This rule was considered fair because certain blokes on certain knot-holes were Dead-eye Richards with an accuracy that could kill any competitive feelings among the other contestants. We tried several handicapping methods, but this entailed so many vital items, with so many permutations, that we floundered in imaginary rules and situations and fell to fighting for the knot-holes, anyway. Three fighting for the possession of one knot-hole. Only one of that three can use that knot-hole, what then? It did not matter which of the three used that particular hole. Their one idea was to stop the other good bloke from using it. Some contestants had a small advantage over the others: the tallest had the choice of more knot-holes.

Such a long struggle to commence a game, you may think. If one has been 'saving' for over an hour the struggle is never long, I can assure you.

At last . . . With heels in line with the narrow grass verge we would wait for the Judge's order to commence. The Judge would stand at the end of the line and meticulously observe that all heels were in line.

'Back a bit, Herby . . . Back a bit, Ticker . . . '

'Hurry up, will 'ee?—I'm just about burstin' here!'

'Wait for it . . . Here, Daylight, me son. Move up a bit . . . Still too far back . . . Bit more . . . Here! You'm feelin' a bit boastful, ain't 'ee?— Move up a bit!'

'Oh, do thee hurry up!—I can't hang on much longer!'

'Tie a knot in un, then!'

'Alright then ... Everybody get ready ... All ready? ... Shoot ... Bang ... FIRE!'

'Coooooooooooooooohhhhhhhh ...'

'Oooooooooooooooohhhhhhhh ...'

'Dear, oh dear, I ... Lovely, ain't it?'

'Oh, blow!—I can't "goo" now!'

'Aaaaaaaaaaaaaahhhhhhhhh ...'

The one with least amount of splash was declared the winner.

I remember the occasion when Ticker's big brother was Judge. He caught Tubb cheating. Namely: 'Did commit an act to the prejudice and good order of an ancient game, in that he did piddle at the foot of the fence, and in doing so, did leave one self-selected knot-hole in the afore-said fence in a one hundred per cent dry condition.'

Retribution always came quickly.

The Judge gave Tubb a shove, pushing him flat against the freshly creosoted fence and followed up with a good stiff knee to the buttocks. What you imagine *could* have happened, did not—mainly due to the theory of angled elevation, but Tubb *did* get a liberal amount of creosote on 'his'. It brought tears to eyes, and didn't he holler? We almost died with laughter.

True—a brisk burnish from the ever faithful dock leaf may well have been the answer, but they were in short supply at this time of the year.

> In dock—out sting.
> Docks is good for everythin'.

On our way up-town we would try to console the doubled-up, knock-kneed-walking straight-armed, fist-clenched, moaning Tubb, but we were always beaten with fits of uncontrollable laughter. Poor old Tubb whimpered like a well-beaten pup. We passed his home on the way, but he declined to go indoors in case his mother asked him 'what was up'.

We arrived at the Market Place on-Cross where we herded him to the horse trough and huddled about him to conceal him from the curiosity of the many passers-by whilst he carried out his ablutions. We tittered and sniggered as the whimper grew to an agonised moan ... We laughed as the moan developed to a teeth-gritting groan of sheer agony ... The final gasping, strangled scream sent us deliriously into fits of hoopying and hollering and spates of hilarious belly laughter ...

There must have been at least a half inch of ice on that horse trough.

End of the Line

I shall now tell you another couple of small 'rozzims' (yarns), if I may.

A few years before I came along, Our Gramf had to deliver two
crates of rifles to the Drill Hall and, because the entrance to the Drill
Hall yard necessitated the negotiation of a very steep slope and a sharp
right-turn, Gramf decided to lift the extra burden from Oliver's
shoulders and pulled him up alongside the front wall of the Drill Hall
which faced the Main Road.

From there, he pushed the crates over the wall, but the second one
slipped and fell and scattered the rifles over the yard. The crate could
not be closed properly after the rifles had been replaced inside, so Gramf
took his 'tar-paully-in' from the waggon and was in the act of wrapping
the broken case in this when a sergeant of the Territorials arrived.

He brandished a revolver and accused Gramf of being a member of
the I.R.A.

He refused to listen to reason . . .

. . . so Gramf gave him one of his renowned right-handed, upper-
cutting, 'tiddy-mashers' and knocked him out.

End of story . . .

Little Eddard Billick was bad in bed, and he lived with his folks in a
little house down by the Railway Station.

Not too far away in another part of town a man had moved into his
'new' house. He was Somerset, but was also a 'foreigner' (outside our
area) and had only been in residence about six months, so the residents
had not started to converse with him very much.

His garden and orchard was surrounded with a high galvanized-iron
fence. As he emerged from his back door he saw a young'un stealing his
Beauty of Baths and gave chase. The young'un dodged him easily amongst
the trees, but the man was not worried about this because he knew he
could catch him the minute he attempted to climb the high fence. The
young'un must have realized this as well, so he nipped in through the
open back door, through the passage, and out through the open front
door!

173

This upset the Apple Man, so he 'called-Copper'. He knew where the young'un lived, and together they went to the home in question. Big Ted, little Eddard Billick's father, answered the door. Why they called him Big Ted, I do not know, because he was only about six foot and never weighed more than eighteen stone. He quietly listened to the complaint and then took them to the bedside of Little Eddard.

'Is that he?' he asked them.

'Ah, that's he!' the Apple Man replied.

'Can't be!' said Big Ted. 'He've been bed for the last three days!'

' Get out of it!' shouted the Apple Man. 'I do know a Burrows when I see one!'

The Copper then realized that, even if the Apple Man had the wrong young'un, there was still some probable room for thought on the name of the other, and hadn't there often been cases of mistaken identity between Little Eddard and Our Young'un (four-down)? He decided to take the investigation a little further.

It was here that local knowledge took an important part. It was half-past opening time. The weather was 'main drowthy' (thirsty weather). It was not a working day, so follow your nose to the nearest pub to our house . . . enter that pub . . . listen for the voice of bad language and argument . . . and he found Our Vather first time!

Vather immediately became silent and docile on being approached by our pair of investigators. Normally, the Apple Man would have been met with derisive remarks, oaths and empty threats, and this sudden change of behaviour could not be truly attributed to the presence of the uniform because they, too, had worn the scorch marks of Vather's drunken wrath.

No . . . This particular Copper was a hard nut . . . Ex-Army Heavy-weight Boxing Champion . . . Twice Somerset Constabulary Heavy-weight Boxing Champion . . . and was just as much at home in a brawl or a street fight. He was known as 'Ginger' throughout Somerset, and he placed Vather well down on his mental list of trouble-makers capable of giving him any form of physical apprehension.

Vather listened . . . As he did so, he sipped his cider with the airs of a drunken judge. As the Apple Man neared the end of his story of woe, Vather, smiling blissfully, slowly raised his face to the ceiling and shook his head from side to side like a barn owl on the lookout.

'What do'ee mean, no?' the Apple Man asked.

'Well, it do show thee, don't it?' Vather explained. 'It can't be none of my tribe, 'cos they do only get blamed when *nobody*–don't see *nobody—doin'* what's been done!'

Ginger considered this fair comment and so retired with his unworthy witness. Ginger was also aware that Vather 'didn't never listen to nobody not for long' during 'office hours'.

Now—take that period of time from when Gramf stopped his horse and cart beside the Drill Hall wall, to when Ginger and the Apple Man walked out of the pub. Throughout that period we were known—and recognized for what we were. We made our mark.

Glastonbury has been around from the year 'dot'. Compare our mark with the long line of the town's history and fame, and we would appear as the most minute speck. Take each, and every one of those tiny, insignificant specks from that line, and you would have a long, long line of nothing.

Our Mother wonders why I insist on raking up the past . . .

'Usin' all they daft old words . . . I do wonder where you do get um from at times. Folk around here is beginnin' to think you'm a bit of a "funnyossity"!'

. . . and I wonder *why* Mother wonders.

Those 'good old days' were the 'bad days' and the 'hard days' . . . I wouldn't like to see them return, yet I am proud and pleased to have been a part of them. The true value of all things are not fully realized until they are going, or gone. Has this something to do with it?

For the future, there is hope . . . For the present, there is existence to consider . . . The past has made me what I am—the only definite subject of the three.

Was the grass greener in those days with Gramf?

Were things changing so much?

I had seen an auto-gyro flying with a propellor on the top . . . There was another ordinary aeroplane flying with it—a Gloucester Gladiator, I think it was . . . It had a message flying from its tail—something about a Flying Circus down Weston, I think . . .

They had to wait for another year because we had already had our day's holiday down Burn'um.

I had seen pictures of sea-planes with long floats instead of wheels . . . On fag-cards, I think they were . . . Yes, that was it!—There was also a picture of an aeroplane with single wings and no propellor!

You don't have to believe that . . . It was only a fag-card.

There was talk—talk about us having another war with Germany, if we didn't watch-out . . . What?—With our Empire—and our Navy?—They wouldn't dare!

Makes you laugh just to think about it, doesn't it?

—Might just as well have talked about flying to the moon!